LIVING WITH THE DEAD

Mary Martina Dockter

ISBN 978-1-959895-97-8 (paperback)
ISBN 978-1-959895-99-2 (eBook)

Printed in the United States of America

WESTPOINT
PRINT AND MEDIA

DEDICATED TO THOSE
WHO HAVE GONE BEFORE US
MAY THEY FIND PEACE

LIVING WITH THE DEAD

You're in your home, thinking you're alone.
As the wind howls, outside like a low groan.
You'll hear creeping of footsteps by the bed.
It is then you pull the covers over your head.

For the dark of night is when they will roam.
A scary sight when shadow souls cry a moan.
From the underworld but they're here instead.
You're in your home and living with the dead.

2023

BOOK ONE

THE DAUNTING

THE DAUNTING

An intimidating shiver, creeps up your spine.
When dealing with fear's anticipation design.
For what is unseen, may not be for your eyes.
As there is a veil between dimensions is wise.
A spiritual world will make a presence known.
To those open to believe, in the hidden shown.

2023

"THE DEAD ARE LIVING AS WELL
IN HEAVEN ON EARTH AND HELL"
M.M.D

CHAPTER 1

I don't see dead people, like in the movie SIXTH SENSE with the actors Bruce Willis who played the phantom psychiatrist who is unaware he died and Haley Joel Osment, his young and gifted patient who actually did see the deceased with his own eyes, but I do have a sixth sense when it comes to feeling their presence around me.

I have felt their energy ever since I was a little girl. I knew there was something very different about me. I couldn't put a finger on it. Some will probably say, it's just a tiny tyke's lively imagination, but even back then I believed in my heart I was somehow being touched by the spiritual world.

They are here living among us. Well, I wouldn't actually say living. It's more like coexisting. We are unable to see them because of a hidden veil; a shroud to keep us apart. However, there are portals within this thin cloth that some have passed through and these lost souls are ghosts.

Are they lost? I don't think so. Wouldn't you try to find your way back home? I can't imagine, one minute you're here and in a blink of an eye you're not. Just because you leave this earthly place doesn't' mean you leave behind all your thoughts and emotions. The very being of your existence goes with you and that desire for living is within every inch of you; even when you're dead. That is why we have apparitions.

That is why they try to communicate. How hard it must be to not be able to express what is happening to you. Where's my body? It's like being old, but your mind is still spry. No wonder children and animals are spirit lightning rods. The essence of life drips from them like dew drops.

And that is the reason they cling to me. From the day I was born I danced. You see, I only weighed 2lb. 14oz. That didn't stop me. My parents said my arms and legs wouldn't stop moving and kicking. I took the bottle, bigger than me, like a champ. They knew I was going to make it because I was full of life. In other words I was a visitant's energy source.

"A PARALLEL UNIVERSE IS OF A TWIN
A MIRROR IMAGE MY LIFE TO BEGIN"
M.M.D

CHAPTER 2

I am a twin! My internal yoke sister and I have a special bond. There is a magnetic, mind force between us. We can sense and sometimes even read each others thoughts. For many years there have been Twin Studies conducted on identical and fraternal twins. The research is a key tool in discovering the importance of environmental over genetic influences. I can tell you right now, it's all in the genes!

The spiritual realm connects with this energy. Our minds are already open to their dimensional presence. We're like a conduit between universes. A shortwave radio receiver to the other side. However, that doesn't mean every twin is connected to this unique radiotelephone. It's a special gift!

Or curse! It is how one looks at it. I, for one, do not take it for granted. That is why I've decided to document my experiences, including those of my family, with the dead; in other words, no longer alive, but you see, I believe that definition is wrong. They are alive. They have a soul, just not a body.

Who are we to say they don't exist. That's like saying, "extraterrestrials don't exist." There is so much we don't know. There is so much we're not being told by the church and the government. Luckily some, like me, have witnessed these entities. The truth is coming out. No matter how many lies are told facts cannot be buried. I'm thankful for the brave men and women who hunt for honesty. We are not alone. We live in this world with those that have gone before us.

"THERE IS GOOD AND BAD IN US ALL
FROM THE WEE TIKE TO THE TALL"

M.M.D

CHAPTER 3

There's good and bad in all of us. A benevolent being whispers in one ear and a malevolent master in the other. Are they real; as real as you and I! It's a battle since the beginning of time. If you listen very closely, you can hear them arguing back and forth for your soul. It's more like giving a sales pitch!

The younger you are, the more in tune to this bickering you are. You're also more in sync with a person's aura; their life light. It's a field of energy surrounding a physical body. Everyone illuminates different colors that affect mood and an emotional state. These hues will even transmit your state of mind onto others.

As a child I could see these brilliant flashes of light. I didn't know what they were, but I knew when to avoid a grown-up. Especially a next door neighbor that reeked with pure dark energy. She was as callous as a trained pit bull for a dog fight. Her daughter was on that same leash too. So, when my other half would go over to play, our mother had no idea she was being bullied. I, on the other hand, avoided them like the plague.

My sister wasn't tortured in the sense of the word. She didn't have any physical scars. However, that mean mom made it quite clear my twin was beneath her and her daughter; like an insect that needed to be squashed.

My sister hated milk. It physically made her gag, but that monster of a mother didn't care. One day, when my sis ate lunch with them, that mom practically poured it down her throat. All the while lecturing how healthy it was and how bad our mom was because she didn't make her drink the white stuff.

That day I tried listening to both sides on my shoulder. Believe me, my celestial conscience begged me not to do it, but I wasn't hearing it. Not with my twin sister crying her heart out over what just happened. I truly felt her pain. The pain was so real that I only heard my angel's nemesis say, "It's time for revenge!"

Have you ever played King of the Hill? It was my turn to rule the roost. The devil of a daughter began taunting me, "I'm the king of the hill. Try knocking me off my throne." It was an invitation I gladly accepted, but she didn't know I had company accompanying me. I felt anger's power, overpower me. Maybe I was possessed!

I knocked her off the hill alright. I knocked the living daylights out of her. I punched her like Ralphie punching Scott "Scut" Farkus in a "Christmas Story". The difference, my mom wasn't there to pull me off to save her. When the beating was over, she was a bloody mess. It felt so good to kick her_____. You know what I mean.

Where there's sweet revenge there's consequences. She ran home beaten and bruised. Of course, her mom tried to find me to kill me, but I'm a pretty good hider. I could see this mad, wretch of a woman search for me in vain. And Oh boy, I could hear her curse me. She screamed, "You can't hide forever. I'm gonna catch you and beat you like you did my daughter."

I think my guardian angel forgave me and saved me because I never got horsewhipped. I didn't even get a spanking at home. My twin accomplice must have told mom about the milk escapade and my mischievous antics. I'm guessing that put the kibosh on any jail time. You see, ma had a little fire in her too. She doesn't let anyone walk or talk over her. Especially, someone who had an aura of unfiltered, putrefied meanness!

"A HOUSE IS LIVING AND BREATHING
WITH THE SOULS OF THOSE GRIEVING"
M.M.D

CHAPTER 4

Just like people, inanimate objects can be possessed. They become a living vessel for the un-living, a breath of fresh air for the un-breathing. In other words, a home for the homeless. Our grandparents' house was such a dwelling.

When you're a kid, your grandpa and grandma's pad is a haven for foolery. You literally can get away with murder. Well, not in the actual sense of killing, but for example; eating candy before supper. Or in my case, smoking a cigar with grandfather and drinking beer with grandmother. Because of their laxly enforced parental rules, I can thank them for me being a non-smoker and a non-drinker today. Although in reality, my grandparents were very wholesome.

"Cleanliness is next to Godliness", and when it comes to housecleaning our mother's mom was a goddess. Her house was clean as a whistle and so were her grandkids; inside and out. The stairs going up to the washroom was a trek into uncharted territory. As soon as you stepped unto the landing a feeling of being watched had the hair on your arms saluting at attention. Your eyes glance back and forth hoping to get a peek at what's peeking at you. I never felt comfortable taking baths in that bathroom; especially with disembodied spirits watching. I can tell you, there's no resting, just testing of wits!

The spacious, second floor transmitted a spooky aura. Our grandparents' bedroom was creepy. I could swear I heard children crying. Thank goodness a crucifix was hanging between their beds. It became a beacon of light for the leery. Something is surely lurking within its chamber walls. Whatever is in the house took up residence upstairs. Even the guest bedroom was bedeviled.

I can imagine you're thinking this child is imagining things. Like I said previously, children and animals can sense the senseless. These childhood experiences, liken cattle being branded, are stitched in every fiber of my being. The memories are still daunting to this day!

"WHAT FUN IS THERE IN BEING CLEAN
YOU NEED MUD ON YOUR FACE TO BE SEEN"
M.M.D

CHAPTER 5

Spending time at our grandparents was like Halloween with its trick or treats. There were many wonderful treats, but with the good comes the bad. Our grandmother was a little, ole German lady. I can see her, even now, wearing a flower, print dress with stockings and black, patent leather shoes with wide heels for stomping. It was her daily uniform!

Remember in the last chapter when I mentioned her grandkids being as clean as a whistle inside and out. A better motto would have been; "better out than in," and the perfect place to pull off her diabolical debauchery was in the kitchen with its stainless steel table.

Let me set the scene for you. The kitchen table chairs are pushed aside making an easy access to a toilet close by. A fresh batch of towels are surgically placed on the table top's surface, where some kind of mid-evil apparatus is used to give out ENEMAS, like candy, to white as ghost grandchildren. To this day, I have a hard time looking at a vintage, stainless steel, kitchen table without feeling constipated.

Grandma was a hoot! When playing outside, we'd inevitably find newly hatched baby birds. One time my eldest brother found a small chick flapping on the sidewalk. He tried catching the tiny warbler, but to his horror grandma stomped the hatchling flat as a pancake.

Yep! That's our grandmother. She's a no, nonsense kind of a gal. Looking back, she was ahead of her time. Those enemas kept us from getting deathly sick when a lot of childhood diseases were going around, but still, standing in line to get an enema was not a joy ride and watching a helpless, infant fowl stomped to death, literally, are what nightmares come from.

Hearing our grandmother's life story made me realize why she's the way she is. As I mentioned earlier, I am a twin. I'm from a long line of twins. Our mom's mom had two sets of twin boys, but only one baby boy lived. I can't even imagine the pain she must have gone through.

Three sons are searching for their mother. Maybe that is why the sound of children crying, echoed in our grandparents' bedroom. And maybe, just maybe, the sight of siblings taking a bath, mentioned in the previous chapter, reminds the threesome of the warm amniotic fluid within a mother's womb. I can only convey what I have felt and heard. My wish is that they had been reunited with my grandmother, their mother, at the time of her untimely death.

"WINGS OF AN ANGEL A FLICKER OF LIGHT
A GUIDING PRESENCE IN THE DARK OF NIGHT"
M.M.D

CHAPTER 6

What you think you've seen may not be what you see. Or maybe it's something not meant to be seen. The dead, for the most part, do not wish to be detected. They go about their business just like you and me. They also become startled when spooked! So you see, seeing a ghost is very uncommon, but the uncommon can become the common; especially when sleeping upstairs in your grandparents ghostly, guest room.

The flicker of car lights can play tricks on you. When there are no cars about, it could be something else. Something of the supernatural! Orbs are spheres of white light or even different shades of color. People believe these celestial formations represent the presence of angels. While others think they could be extraterrestrial in nature. Either way, entities are using the power of light to travel to our earthly dimension.

These spirits are electromagnetic energy fields. They contain an angelic power source enabling them to appear to humans. Their circular shapes represent unity, wholeness and eternity. However, what if, they are not angelic. What if it's a fallen angel with a demonic energy. Satan tries to deceive people by appearing in the form of brilliant, illuminating light. You should never feel fear when seeing an orb. If you do, it's a good indication it's not a benevolent being.

When you're a kid, seeing anything out of the ordinary will conjure up fear. We know keeping a closet door closed or not letting an arm or a leg dangle off the bed is an insurance policy against the perils of the boogeyman. So, when I see balls of light strategically floating in the room, I'm not thinking angels or demons. I'm thinking, get me the heck out of here.

Fear is a mysterious emotion. When your mind tells you to run, but your body is frozen stiff; all you can do is watch and pray. Let me tell you, I did a lot of watching and praying when staying overnight at my grandparents.

**"DON'T QUESTION WHAT YOU MAY SEE
WHEN YOUR HEART TELLS YOU TO BELIEVE"**

M.M.D

CHAPTER 7

There is one unexplained incident that happened in the upstairs bedroom that I'm still trying to understand. To this day, it continues to resonate in the depths of my soul and forever haunts me. I try to make some kind of sense out of it, but there is no common sense about it at all. What I encountered was truly out of the ordinary. A conundrum to its very core; a visitant vision!

All I remember is sitting on the top bunk and thinking to myself, "How did I get here?" I was by myself and none of my siblings were nearby. I had no recollection of being put to bed. It was like my memory was erased. I sat there in darkness in complete silence. I was all alone. So I thought!

As I was trying to figure out what was going on, I saw three figures wearing hooded robes just staring at me. I stared right back at them. They were not very tall; maybe three feet in length and their outfits glistened like stars. I wasn't afraid, just baffled! What's happening? Where's my family? Who are you guys? And why do I have the uneasy feeling you're the ones who put me in bed? Before I could say a word, they're gone. I was downstairs dazed and confused.

Now, I'm thinking, "How did I get here?" I don't remember walking down those stairs. There's no rhyme or reason to any of this.

It plays over and over in my head. I've come up with a couple of theories about the apparitions. My very first instinct was to think they were angels. As I've said before, I have seen orbs in that room and these entities also illuminated light. For the longest time it gave me comfort thinking they're angelic. However, why were they wearing cassocks? So, I started believing they were saints. I'm Catholic and that theory stuck for awhile. Now I'm not too sure that's the ticket. Today I'm more convinced they were most likely space travelers.

I've given this a lot of thought. That room could have been a vortex; a gateway for spirits and extraterrestrials to pass through. I've done research and there is such a thing as hooded aliens. Supposedly they're benevolent. I didn't feel I was in any danger or harm, just mystified. Maybe they read my mind and I was asking way too many questions and they wanted to get the heck out of there. I'm sure they didn't expect me to be sitting up and staring at them. For dam sure, I wasn't expecting to be staring at them either. I'm hoping someday I'll get answers to my questions because it won't be the last time I'm visited or abducted by something not from this Earth.

"I'LL SLEEP WHEN I'M DEAD
FOR THERE'S TOO MUCH AHEAD"
M.M.D

CHAPTER 8

What goes up must come down; downstairs for that matter. Our grandparents' home embodied an unfinished black hole. I call it that because it was dark and eerie. It's the perfect place for kids to play and the perfect place for spirits to play also.

My sister and I hated taking naps. It was a given that right after lunch my mother and grandparents would take a snooze. Of course, they wanted us to fall asleep with them. Yeah right, as soon as they started snoring we snuck out of there and got as far away as we could. We didn't want to take the chance of waking them up so we hid in the abyss.

Just like upstairs, you get a feeling that something is watching you in the dungeon. I never played down there by myself, but with a sidekick sister fears are lessened and your guard is off. Having fun overrules and then stranger danger things can inevitably happen.

In the comer of the cemented corridor was a passage leading to a cellar. The door was made of very old, rotting wood. It was always locked which made it even more intriguing. So, when it was left opened, by mistake, of course I had to investigate. My twin was too busy horsing around to notice I had disappeared exploring. As soon as I entered the cellar my only exit slammed shut behind me. I shrieked, "WHO CLOSED THE DOOR?" I was too scared to find out. I quickly opened the door and ran to my sis acting like nothing was wrong. I didn't tell her what I just witnessed. Come to think of it, I never told her about the so called aliens until we were much older. I kept most of what was happening between me, myself and I.

Even though I've experienced the supernatural I've never felt threatened. My grandmother and mother were very religious and as Catholic Christians they held in their possession a secret weapon; the Holy Rosary. These sacred beads were a gift to humanity from the Blessed Virgin Mary. She appeared to three, young Portuguese children and taught them how to say the prayers of the prayer beads. It is our belief that saying the rosary helps fight against evil. Thank God my mom and grandmother prayed the rosary everyday!

So you see, it's like having "Ghostbusters" from the movie protecting me with an invisible force field. It's a good thing because phantoms are everywhere and they can follow you wherever you go.

"WORRY NEVER WINS
WHEN PRAYING BEGINS"

M.M.D

CHAPTER 9

We lived in Oak Ridge, Tennessee during our formative years. It was a magical and enchanting time when I was young, but it was also mysterious and daunting. Something lurked in the air; a heaviness you could just feel. Maybe that is why we played outside all the time. As a rug rat, having to be indoors was like being tortured. There's a freedom exploring in the wilderness; free from pain and worry.

You're probably thinking, "You're a kid, what do you have to fret about." I agonized over everything! I'm sure I was a hypochondriac because if I heard about a disease, I imagined I had it. I even wrote to my aunt telling her I thought I was pregnant. How silly! I was only about eight and hadn't even reached puberty yet, but none the less, I lost sleep over it. Worry was an entity trying to take control of my life at a very immature age.

I really don't think a demonic being was trying to possess me. Or maybe it was! It's a fact that light and darkness dwells among the living. Most of us are not even aware that a spiritual warfare is going on. Eventually, I conquered my disturbed distress over stupid stuff by praying. All the while, an ominous presence continued lurking in my life, stalking me like a werewolf. Maybe that is why our mother pinned medals of the Miraculous Virgin Mary on our undergarments. They're like a bullet shield against the evil one.

In fact, our mom had a slew of weapons ready for the fight; holy water, holy cards, the lighting of candles in church and novenas to name a few. And don't forget the atomic bomb of Catholic artifacts; the rosary beads of prayer. She was always ready to whip out a sacramental memento like a gunslinger. It's a good thing because we recently received a nefarious gift from who knows who. I have no recollection where it came from. It was more like a curse though. My siblings and I were intrigued and captivated by it. In our possession we had an Ouija board. And we weren't afraid to use it!

"A GAME OF DEATH NEVER BE PLAYED
YOUR LIFE BE FORSAKEN AND GRAVED"

M.M.D

CHAPTER 10

There's no playing an Ouija board, it plays you! It's not a child's toy, but a tool for the dead! Did you know that nobody really knows the origin of this mystic, board game? When the makers of the first official product asked the board what it should be called, it spelled out "Ouija". Then they wanted to know what that meant. Its reply was, "Good Luck". What the heck does that mean! I'm thinking enter at your own risk!

The game consists of a flat board with letters of the alphabet arranged in two semi-circles above the numbers O thru 9 and the words "yes" and "no" in the uppermost corners of the board and "goodbye" at the bottom. The premise of the gambit was for two or more victims to sit around the plank, place their finger tips on the poltergeist like planchette and ask a question then watch the device spell out an answer. We didn't know how dangerous the talking board could be, but we would soon find out!

To make matters worse, we didn't play the game in the safety of our home, but in a dark and vacant basement. I wouldn't even call it a basement, but a crawl space under an abandoned house. The only light was a candle flickering and casting shadows on the walls. We were spellbound kids playing with fire and asking questions to who knows what. Did we, unknowingly, open up a portal?

Shadow people are phantomlike entities that appear out of nowhere. They are black, disembodied specters floating through the air. Often times, they can be seen out of the corner of your eye. That is how I have witnessed them. However, sometimes they make their presence known in full bloom. It's at night when they're most active because usually the living are asleep, but there are times when that's not the case.

Take for example my younger, oldest brother who sees them coming into his bedroom. They glide through the air and hover near him. Of course he pretends to be sleeping as he watches them levitate. Who are they? What do they want? Did we open a door for them to come in by playing the game? "Good luck" is the perfect name when trying to get answers to those questions. I just pray we didn't allow a more sinister spirit, than the shadow people, into our lives.

"AN INNER VOICE YOU MAY HEAR
RIGHT FROM WRONG AND WHAT YOU FEAR"

M.M.D

CHAPTER 11

Fear itself is a mechanizism from the devil. You're drowning in a sea of despair with its dark energy. I felt this evil around me. Sometimes it would even speak to me. Not in the actual sense of speaking, but a feeling of death. Yes, death! It was like the grim reaper was whispering in my ear that something bad was going to happen to me. I was scared to death!

One time the feeling was so strong that I broke my silence and told my mom. It wasn't the best time to tell her because mom and dad were getting ready to go out for dinner. I begged her to please stay home because something bad was going to happen. I didn't know what I just felt I was going to die. As you can imagine, that didn't go over very well. They did go out to dinner and as you can see, I didn't die, but my mother did!

It was years later when I was only fourteen. To this day, I truly believe I was reading the message wrong. I was feeling death, not mine, but hers. It's not easy for me to admit this. Maybe I could have saved her if I would have been more in tune to what I was feeling. It never dawned on me that it wasn't me. I'd give anything to go back in time and tell her to please see a doctor because she would have nose bleeds for no apparent reason. If they had caught the brain tumor in time, our lives definitely would have been completely different.

I loved our mother very much. After she died it was hard to imagine that she would never see her children grow and become successful adults. She would never be there when her children got married and have her grandbabies. Now that I am older, I believe she did see all those special events in our lives. She's always been here with us in spirit!

"IF A TREE COULD TALK WHAT WOULD IT SAY
NOTHING IT HAS SEEN TOO MUCH TO CONVEY"
M.M.D

CHAPTER 12

At this point of my story our mother is still with us. She is among the living with flesh on bones and blood running through her veins. Thank goodness because she is the cornerstone of our family. We love her dearly!

It's strange being able to sense the future. I can't predict what will happen, I just feel it. Take for example our next door neighbor's crabapple tree. I was having a bewildering premonition about this overgrown shrub in their yard. Something was going to happen with it, to it, by it, I wasn't sure. It was as though the crabapples were trying to tell me bits and pieces regarding its futuristic well-being, but a tree can't talk and even if it could. I don't speak tree. All I know is I felt it was crying.

Soon after that the accident occurred. Mom and my two younger brothers were in the car ready to leave when she hears the phone ringing in the house. Mom tells them to, "Stay put and don't touch anything." Of course, the youngest climbs into the front seat and starts pretending he's a racecar driver. Only to our horror, he really does become a racecar driver!

The want-to-be dragster puts the car in neutral and it starts rolling down the street. His older brother jumps ship and makes it to safety leaving his stuntman brother going down with the ship. If it wasn't for the wheels that were turned towards the curb, I would be writing about a completely different scenario, but luckily, the automobile drove into a sacrificial lamb; the crabapple tree. The vehicle and the tree trunk were the only casualties. Our brothers came out of the wreckage without a scratch, although they both were plagued with nightmares. The instigator of the incident started stuttering and sleepwalking right after the mishap. Our poor mother was ridden with guilt and did penance; praying and thanking God for keeping her little boys safe.

There must be something about our next door neighbor's residence that gave me a strange feeling when I was in their yard. To top it off, they even had monkey bars in their backyard. A contraption of steel made for climbing. It was a kid magnet. I for one was drawn to it even though it kept telling me to be careful. Did I listen? No, like a chimp I would swing upside down without a care in the world. I had no idea my world was about to break.

My arm that is! Like a dummy, I announced at the top of the playground equipment my intentions of doing a backwards flip. If I would have landed this feat, I could have been in the Olympics. Instead I landed on my arm. I knew I broke it because I heard the snap of bones. Why didn't I listen to my intuition? And to make matters worse, mom and dad weren't home. I had to sit in our friend's house with a towel over my broken appendage to keep their mother from fainting. It made her sick just looking at the nearly, compound fracture.

So you see, those feelings of seeing the future were real to me. I had a gift, only I didn't know how to read it. Feeling the future and seeing the future are completely different. I'm hoping one day I'll get a visual to go with it. Maybe I should be careful what I wish for. Knowing the future has great responsibilities and is nothing to fool around with. It's meant to stay a secret until it's the present. At this present moment, I have enough to deal with when it comes to spirits, the supernatural and Catholic School. Especially, when I'm being bullied by a nun!

**"FAITH IS WHAT YOU MAKE OF IT
IT IS WITHIN THERE'S NO FAKING IT"**

M.M.D

CHAPTER 13

Just because you wear a religious habit doesn't mean you're in the habit of being nice to children. My siblings and I went to parochial schools growing up and let me tell you, you grow up pretty fast when attending a Catholic institution. There's a no, nonsense policy when dealing with nuns. If you're lucky, a nice one might be thrown into the mix, but for the most part they rule with an iron fist or a perforated wooden paddle in my case.

Personally, I never met the holiest of holes, but a couple of times I did come close to being introduced to its wrath. For some reason, nuns and I didn't click. It never made any sense to me how they could be so religious and at the same time be so cruel to their students. I don't think they liked kids. In their eyes, they see little devils. Had they forgotten what Jesus said? He said, "Let the little children come to me." In His eyes we are little angels. In reality, we're angels and devils and that is how it should be.

Even though I've had some bad experiences with nuns, I still believe in my Catholic faith. It gives me comfort knowing there are special priests appointed by their bishops to perform exorcisms. An exorcism means "binding by oath". It is a spiritual or religious ritual expelling a demon from a person, an object, or a specific place that is believed to be possessed. As a child, I desperately wanted to talk to our parish priest about what I was feeling, but every time I went to confession I'd chicken out. I'm sure he was only use to hearing the normal venial sins a kid would say in the confessional. "I talked in school" or "I hit my brother or sister." You know normal kid stuff. Not, "I think I'm possessed!" Although, it would have been funny to see his facial expression after hearing that one.

It didn't help not having the tell tale signs of being possessed like talking in a foreign tongue without any prior knowledge of that language, spewing out vomit, head spinning around, unusual human strength or knowing someone's prior, personal history. I'm sure I would have been ridiculed for an overactive imagination and banned from going to confession for awhile. The nuns would have had a hay day hearing that one. I just hope and pray what's said to the priest stays with the priest. And God, of course!

"LOOK BEYOND WHAT YOU MAY SEE
MAY NOT BE A VISION FOR OTHERS TO BELIEVE"
M.M.D

CHAPTER 14

I never could fathom why my twin wanted to be a nun when she grew up. Although, she did possess some of their characteristics; being bossy and a desire to serve God. As a kid, she took it a little further and became a priest by hearing our confessions in the laundry closet and saying Mass in our bathroom. She stood in the tub handing out wafers of smashed bread for communion as we knelt before the pretend communion rail. At that age, she was willing to be among the ranks of the religious. Her one wish was to become a nun.

Not me! So when our friend from school wanted a sleepover, I'd stay home. Why, because she wanted to be a nun too. What kind of pajama party was that? Instead of nightgowns, they wore nun outfits. The highlight of their evening was praying the rosary. Don't get me wrong, I pray the rosary, but not at a time when you're suppose to be having fun; not being a NUN!

On one occasion when they were piously praying, a vision appeared to them. They were kneeling beside the bed when three rosaries in the shape of a cross hovered above their heads on the wall. Of course, they were frightened and tried to tum the light on. The light switch was dead and they were left in the dark staring at the glowing apparition until it disappeared. Mesmerized, they thanked God for giving them a sign. They believed the Blessed Virgin Mary was sending them a message to keep their diligence in praying the holy beads. On Monday they were so excited to tell their story to the nuns and priest at our school. Now, I for one believed they truly witnessed what they believed they saw. I went through the same thing when three celestial beings appeared to me, but in their case there's no doubt this was a spiritual, religious vision; not extraterrestrial!

I would have given anything to have witnessed that and you would have thought the Catholic clergy would've been excited too. But no, I think it went over as well as if I'd confessed I was possessed. They didn't want to hear it. I know these two weren't at the level of the Virgin Mary appearing to children at Lourdes, but come on. You'd think the nuns and priest would be happy for them. They swept it under the rug faster than a jackrabbit escaping from a hungry fox. It was never to be spoken of again. I'm sorry, but one never forgets something as monumental as that. I should know!

**"THE GIFT TO BELIEVE MAY BE IN A SIGN
TAKE NOTICE AROUND YOU BY A DESIGN"**

M.M.D

CHAPTER 15

There are signs everywhere and we need only to read them with an open mind. There are angels everywhere and we need only to open our eyes to see them. We are endowed with a special gift at birth; a guardian angel. The belief in tutelary spirits can be traced back to the beginning of time with the patriarch of all such beings; the protector of the church, St. Michael the Archangel. I for one can say. "There is much comfort knowing we are not alone!"

Even though we are unable to see them, there are physical signs indicating they are trying to get our attention. Someone gently stroking your hair, a feeling of warmth throughout your body, a tingling sensation or a strange presence standing at your side is no doubt, your guardian angel.

As I have mentioned earlier, different colored lights often appear. You may even notice sparks of white light or a shadow in your vicinity. Don't be afraid. It is probably your protector. They also appear while you are sleeping. Have you ever had a unique message in your dream? Or better yet, unexplained voices in your ear. It is their way to communicate with the living. They are at our side to give us guidance and to warn us about eminent danger.

My siblings and I borrowed a purple wagon from friends and we were going to ride it down our hilly street. I was in the front with two younger brothers sitting behind me and the youngest of the three plopped in front of me. My sister, who came up with the idea, was not in the wagon, but standing in the back of the dragster ready to give us a humungous push. I knew, right then and there, this was not a good idea. I could see it and hear it. My feet were digging into asphalt not wanting to let us go. In my ear I was hearing, "Don't you do it." In my head I was visualizing a horrendous crash with bodies laying in the street. Exactly what I felt came true. I wasn't able to control the killing machine enough to clear it away from the curb. We hit the sidewalk and the four of us flew like sitting ducks. Luckily a neighbor witnessed the accident and helped with the carnage. I and my brothers were banged up pretty bad. I'm so thankful we survived with only a severe case of road rash. I'm sure our sister was in shock knowing it was mostly her fault. I am manning up and taking some of the blame for the debacle because I was in the driver's seat. I just wish my angel would have been a little louder so my sister could have heard its dire warning too!

"WINGS OF ANGELS LIKE BIRDS IN FLIGHT
ARE THERE TO PROTECT NOT TO FRIGHT"

M.M.D

CHAPTER 16

What if your experience with winged beings is more than a gentle touch or whisper? I have heard of such stories of actual sightings. The one case that made a big impression on me was the "Mothman Prophecy". It is based on true events of a moth like creature terrorizing the residents living in a small town. The premise of the story is whenever the alien looking monster appeared, something tragic was about to happen.

Living in Oak Ridge, Tennessee you come across a variety of different species of wildlife. We spent the majority of our time scavenging the deep, dark woods looking for specimens. As kids we caught our fair share of box turtles and snakes and because of our endeavors our backyard was the neighborhood zoo. I pretty much knew what kind of four-legged or no-legged varmint was out there. Not so much when it came to critters in the air.

I was walking home from visiting a friend down the street taking my time and enjoying the quiet solitude of my own company. I remember, distinctly, there wasn't another living soul around me. All of a sudden, this black as night, winged beast flew above my head and perched itself in a nearby tree. This thing was huge and staring right at me. It was the biggest, dang bird I have ever seen. I didn't feel safe so I ran. I ran as fast as I could. What was that thing? To this day I'm asking that question. There's nothing in the bird kingdom that resembled what I saw. It wasn't a hawk or an eagle. It was way bigger than these birds of prey. That is exactly how I felt; like prey. It almost resembled a human body, but with large wings. When it gazed at me it gave the impression it could read my mind. What type of cryptic creature could it have been? Oak Ridge was the "Secret City" and developed the atomic bomb. Maybe a scientist, back then, developed such a life form resulting from their experimenting with nuclear. Who knows? All I know is, we know nothing when it comes to the black operations of the government and their non-disclosures.

"JUST BECAUSE YOU HAVEN'T SEEN
DOESN'T MEAN THEY HAVEN'T BEAMED"
M.M.D

CHAPTER 17

Since antiquity there have been numerous sightings of cryptic creatures. Those who study cryptology claim they do exist, but in reality, have never proven they're existence. It's kind of a double-edged sword. Although there have been many studies about these things, no one to date has any concrete evidence to back their findings. The saying, "I'll believe it, when I see it," comes to mind.

I still think there are beings out there that are able to evade detection. My siblings and I, on countless occasions, went snake hunting, but never came across a venomous viper. I know for a fact they're slithering in the woods under our noses. Just because we never crossed paths with them doesn't mean they don't exist. The same philosophy should apply to cryptids. It could be they're on a different playing field.

Bigfoot, also called Sasquatch, means "wild men". It's a legend that has been passed down from generation to generation. It is a very large and hairy humanlike beast that roams throughout the forests of North America. There are also countless stories of these creatures around the world. Those who have had the privilege actually witnessing these humanoids should thank their lucky stars because that is where they might be coming from. I believe somewhere out there in the vast universe is their home. To me it just makes common sense.

Think about it, in a lot of cases where sightings of Bigfoot have been documented the presence of orbs or a UFO is noted. Some people have stated that they seem to just disappear out of thin air. One minute they see them, the next they're gone without a trace. It's like these entities walk through an invisible door; a gateway into a cosmic dimension. They've also alleged these half ape, half humans are spirits sent here to protect the Earth to be guardians of nature.

I wonder in actuality if extraterrestrials had a hand in this by cross-breeding apes and humans and what we see or should I say, "don't see" is the end result of their experiments. They do like to abduct and probe their specimens. I wouldn't put it passed them. To the alien we're on the same level as an animal. Why not create a species to spy on mankind and then sent here to snitch on humanity about our nuclear nonsense. Either way, they're of the paranormal. My wish is for someday to be one of the lucky ones to see one!

"TELL ME NO SECRETS TELL ME NO LIES
FOR TRUTH WILL BE TOLD IS REALIZED

M.M.D

CHAPTER 18

Oak Ridge, "The City Behind the Fence" was given this nickname because of the deep, dark secret within its walls. Unbeknownst to many of the residents living in East Tennessee, their small community played a pivotal role in developing the atomic bomb. The township and the country for that matter was unaware of the nation's nuclear activity. Aliens from outer space knew quite well what was going on and aggressively monitored the facility's thermonuclear progression.

It has been documented that extraterrestrials have been fascinated by our military strength for over 75 years. During the Korean War an entire battalion became sick after witnessing a pulsating ray of blue-green light. The soldiers' illness resembled symptoms related to radiation poisoning. U.S. Airmen, during World War II, witnessed unexplained aerial phenomena they labeled as "Foo Fighters". These strange balls of orange lights flew over the French-German border and were a hindrance to the pilots' safety.

So, it doesn't surprise me that UAP's, (Unexplained Aerial Phenomena) have been reported near the Atomic Energy Installation at Oak Ridge. On October 12, 1950 a squadron of eleven or more mysterious objects were spotted on radar traveling across the city's airspace. The declassified FBI files confirmed the tracking and were unable to explain the incident because the city at that time had a "No Fly Zone" policy. To this day our country's weaponry, technology and nuclear power capabilities are being scrutinized by visitors not from this Earth. Are they using these facilities as a fueling station to just gas up? I'm hoping their here to monitor the military, and if need be, intervene if some insane person or country decides to obliterate the human race. I know they have the ability to stop the madness. They've already shut down nuclear missal silos to show what they are capable of. They see us as pawns to be played.

All the while high ranking U.S. military and intelligence personnel try to keep the alien phenomena hidden from the public eye. They think we're gullible enough to believe in their ruse of weather balloons and swamp gas, but too many credible sightings have been reported and there are even more observations, obviously, that have been unreported. Like mine!

"TIME STANDS STILL IN OUTER SPACE
BUT HERE ON EARTH THERE IS NO TRACE"

M.M.D

CHAPTER 19

It was a typical school day and I'm counting down the minutes until lunch and recess. The circular clock above the rectangular, green chalk board is taking its sweet time ticking away. As the theory goes, watching a classroom clock is like watching a pot of water boil. Time just stands still especially when you're sitting in a desk and your stomach is punching you in the gut with hunger pains. Instead of math it sounds like a music class hearing the different instrumental notes being played from the other students' bellies.

Finally the bell rings! In an orderly fashion we stand in a straight line and march to the cafeteria. After the clean plate police examines your lunch tray for anything not consumed because you know there's starving children in China, you're good to go into the next line for recess. My favorite part of the school day!

There's nothing like the freedom of playing in the playground. We can yell to our hearts content and run like a cheetah in the Savanna. The nuns may think they have complete control supervising us at play, but deep within our souls we're untamed. We're the exuberance of life's youthful energy. Eerily you could feel it in the air and so could they. Hovering right above our heads was the unthinkable!

Maybe it was the power of laughter or the vitality of children's liveliness that transmitted a message of welcome. The black as night, triangular craft just floated peacefully in the sky. That wasn't the case on the ground. It was pure pandemonium. The not so saintly sisters acted like the world was coming to an end. They were running around like chickens with their heads cut off. So, of course the students copied the teachers reaction to this awesome, alien attraction. All the while I silently stood in the middle of the chaos staring straight up at the UFO.

I was in awe and transfixed to the point of being hypnotized until a crazed teacher screamed at me to run. BAM! I bolted straight into another kid who was scrambling to find shelter. We butted heads so hard that I blacked out. The next thing I remember is seeing ghost white garments and Catholic School uniforms. A nun told me to get up and run into the school. No empathy here. She didn't even check to see if I was hurt. The way our instructors acted, I can't believe I wasn't left behind to be abducted as a peace offering to the gods.

By the time I woke up the spaceship had vanished. Then the motley mayhem manifested into the classroom. We were told to hide under our desks and stay put. That's all I remember. After that it wasn't mentioned and at the end of the day we were back in our seats staring at the circular clock above the green, rectangular chalk board, counting down the minutes to go home.

It was like nothing had happened. No one said a word about witnessing what we just witnessed. At home my sister and I never told our parents about the best day ever. I wonder if someone or something had a hand in wiping the unidentified aerial phenomena slate clean from memory. It wasn't until years later pieces of the puzzle began to fit together and my mind finally unclassified the supposedly erased memory.

"SEEING IS WITHOUT BELIEVING

BELIEVING IS WITHOUT SEEING"

M.M.D

CHAPTER 20

Never in a million years can I fathom why two little girls who just witnessed a UFO say not a word to their parents or anyone else for that matter about their extraterrestrial experience. It baffles me why the incident was never spoken of in school either. It was like it never happened. But it did!

I am so thankful my twin sister has my back. We both were eye witnesses to this cosmic, triangular craft. Her recollection correlates with mine and no, we didn't dream the same dream. Something mischievous occurred after we were corralled into classrooms and told to hunker down under our desks. I'm just wondering if a black-op government agency had anything to do with erasing evidence. Although I'm thinking it's more likely the men in black or the aliens themselves who telepathically sent a message through the airwaves destroying any footage from our easily manipulated, puny brains. What about the nuns? I'm sure they were more than willing to forget anything of this nature having ever happened. To them their prayers were answered.

Not mine. I want to know if our memories were tampered with for political or military reasons. Maybe what we saw wasn't from outer space. Maybe the government was testing a top secret aircraft and it was in the wrong place at the wrong time. It doesn't make any sense! If they wanted to keep it quiet, why fly over a school yard full of children.

I have many questions, but no answers. If I was zapped, the side effects have definitely worn off because when I shut my eyes I can vividly see a black, triangular object hovering above me. The memory haunts me to this day. Not because I fear it, but because I'm drawn to it. I feel like I'm in that Steven Spielberg movie, "Close Encounters of the Third Kind". I can't explain it, I have an obsession when it comes to UFO's and alien abductions. I'm just like the characters Roy Neary (played by Richard Dreyfuss) and Jillian Guiler (portrayed by Melinda Dillion). I've been chosen!

"NOTERIETY HAS A PRICE
FAME A VIRTUE AND A VICE"
M.M.D

CHAPTER 21

Being of the chosen ones has a price. You're labeled a kook a weirdo. In some cases people have been shunned from society. There are a few empirical accounts that do get notoriety. When I was young I remember hearing about the first alien abduction case publicized in the United States. Of course, I'm talking about Betty and Barney Hill from New Hampshire. I was transfixed to the TV listening to every word as they revealed their chilling ordeal.

It didn't scare me, in fact, I was a little jealous. Even back then I would have given my eye teeth to go on a space ride. I was gonna lose them anyway. They might as well have fallen out for a good cause. And being probed, come on, I'm a pro. Grandma has been training us for years with enemas. I'm sure these so called beings from outer space have more advanced equipment then a stainless steel table, a jar and some tubing. Holy Shit! Anything would have been better than the kitchen from hell.

Some believe extraterrestrials are not from the heavens, but from Satan's abyss. His minions purpose is to confuse humanity. Having us believe we are being abducted when in reality we are being visited by demons. I don't buy that explanation for one minute. It's pretty lame to think mankind is exclusive to the universe. The cosmos has been around for billions of years and we're the only ones to inhabit a planet? Give me a break! No one in their right mind believes that one.

If they're not demons, what are they? Some take another direction and say they are benevolent. I don't think they're angels. No one has ever mentioned wings. I'm coming to the conclusion these things can be both good and bad. There's evil and goodness in people, why can't there be good and bad aliens? I can thank my lucky stars my cosmic visitation was with hooded aliens and not reptilians. Reptilians are a lizard looking humanoid with small, fine scales, a snout and yellowish-green eyes. They have a hostile disposition and regard humans as inferior to their race. Now that's pretty scary!

**"THE SPACE BETWEEN INNER AND OUTER IS REAL
WHEN LIVING ON EARTH THE COSMOS REVEALED"**

M.M.D

CHAPTER 22

What if aliens are not coming from outer space, but from inner space underground. There are first-hand accounts of hypogeum creatures existing within subterrestrial bases on Earth. The most infamous is Dulce Base better known as Nightmare Hall. Supposedly, it is a jointly-operated military and extraterrestrial facility that is under the Archuleta Mesa on the Colorado and New Mexico border near the town of Dulce, New Mexico.

The UFO compound is secretly hidden deep below the surface and situated near the rugged mountains of that area. It is there that diabolical, genetic experiments are being performed on human guinea pigs. Men and women kept in cages are meticulously altered from their original forms with multi-legs and arms creating a new type of species. All in the name of science.

Dulce Base is not the only deal with the devil. The Greada Treaty was a pact with aliens and the United States government where President Dwight D. Eisenhower was to sign an agreement with extraterrestrials for advance technology. In exchange they'd have permission to abduct and perform experiments on minerals, livestock and helpless humans. According to testimony the summit was not successful, but I doubt the creatures from outer space ever got the memo. To this day people are still being abducted and livestock is still being gruesomely, surgically mutilated.

These animals are sadly abandoned after being cruelly abused with laser accurate slices to remove jaws, cow utters and other parts of their lifeless bodies. They're left for dead for the buzzards, but oddly enough no predator will touch their carcass; not even the fierce wolf or mountain lion. Maybe these carnivores can sense the radiation left behind from the unidentified flying object that did this unthinkable, heinous crime.

In some incidents crop circles appear before livestock are found literally cut to pieces. Aliens are known to mark the land with elaborate designs. If only we knew, how to interpret their written language in a farmer's field. It seems they like to brand their conquest like ranchers brand cattle. To them the human race is no different than a four-legged beast. I guess that is why they mark us too!

**"THE MARK OF THE DEVIL HE MAKES
CANNOT BE WASHED OFF BY ONE'S SAKE"**

M.M.D

CHAPTER 23

The mark of the Devil is believed to be a permanent seal that initiates obedience and service to Satan. He created the blemish by scratching his claws across the flesh of a demonic person; usually a witch. It leaves an impression that resembles a blue or red streak from a hot iron. This spot on a body becomes the seal to bind the bargain made for their soul.

The mark of the beast is 666. It is a number that represents man. According to the Bible man and woman were created on the sixth day. During the end times, no one will be able to buy or sell unless they have the mark of the beast. The beast's number is man's number.

The number 777 constitutes a higher power and it's believed to symbolize perfection. The seal of God is His love for humanity. It ensures everlasting protection and verifies your relationship with Him. Like an insurance policy, He will be a shield against evil for believers when the apocalypse comes.

What about the marks left by aliens on the surface of the Earth. Are they symbols initiating obedience and service to them? Are they staking a claim on their property; us? Crop circles are created by UFO's raking their claws across fields of flesh and in some cases the flesh is ours. There are those that have been abducted and have undergone surgical procedures with scars to prove it. Doctors are left baffled when retrieving pieces of metal under the skin of patients claiming to have been abducted. How on Earth did an alloy get there? Well, I'm pretty sure whatever it is, it's not from here. There are those that believe aliens are installing some kind of tracking device to keep an eye on their victims. I wouldn't put it past them.

I also wouldn't put it past extraterrestrials to mark their prey using symbols that resemble crop circles. I know because I have one on my leg. It looks like a tiny ice cream scoop spooned a hole in my limb. One day the indentation wasn't there, the next day it was. I have no idea how it got there. Or maybe I do!

"THE BEGINNING OF TIME DOES NOT BARTER BY THOSE BEFORE US FROM THEIR CHARTER"

M.M.D

CHAPTER 24

Since the beginning of time we have been visited by entities from outer space. The Zuni Indians for example claim their ancestors came from the sky as Star People. They are also referred to as Indigo children; a name given to alien-human hybrids. These astral beings arrived on Earth as extraterrestrials, but eventually became part human.

One can only look back through history and discover hidden signs revealing we are not alone. There are 10,000 year-old rock paintings depicting UFO's and aliens during the stone age. I'm pretty sure a caveman's imagination didn't come up with those illustrations on their own.

What about biblical ancient paintings from famous artists portraying unusual images of flying saucers. It's not something a renaissance painter from the 15th century would put on a canvas unless the depiction had been actually seen. There are too many portraits from antiquity of unidentified flying objects and creatures from outer space to dismiss their existence.

Visitors from beyond our universe have been with us forever. It only makes sense these non-human beings kept a record of some kind on whom they've abducted. What better way then to follow a gene pool from the same family. It is well documented that a parent that's been chosen for an alien examination will most likely pass the curse onto their child. It's almost like a family tradition to be abducted.

What if there is no recollection of a parent or sibling experiencing a visitation. The only uninvited guests my brother ever witnessed were of shadow people. They may be of the supernatural, but they're not from another planet. Remember my twin sister who also observed the UFO at our school. She's never mentioned any side effects from the triangular craft's sighting. Nope, I can't think of anybody else that's been earmarked for a ride. Maybe I'm first in line in my family to be taken!

"THERE'S NO BETTER FAIRYTALE THAN LIFE WITH ALL OF ITS WONDER AND STRIFE"

M.M.D

CHAPTER 25

Oak Ridge, Tennessee was the perfect living embodiment of a fairytale childhood. My siblings and I ruled the roost in our neighborhood. We had free reign to ride bicycles in the streets. Better yet, explore the dark, dense woods in our vast, wide open backyards. Nothing could possibly topple our little kingdom. Foolishly, that is what we thought.

Like a ton of bricks the news of our family moving knocked me for a loop. I had no clue our father, who was in the Army, volunteered to go to Vietnam. Why should I know, I was just a kid. So, of course the rest of the household was drafted to Kentucky to be closer to our mother's relatives. It was a bitter sweet situation. The Secret City will surely be missed, but on the bright side we'll be calling the Bluegrass State home once again.

The wheels of making a dramatic life change was in motion and the day of the departure came without a hitch. Well, I wouldn't exactly say that. My dad pinky swore I could take my parakeet with us, but at the last minute reneged on his promise and gave my precious Cookie to neighbors. I was devastated to the point I became deathly ill. It's amazing how quickly I came down with tonsillitis. Instead of a small, insignificant bird in the car, my parents had to deal with a sick rug rat. There's nothing like sweet revenge!

I don't remember much of the ride. I do have flashbacks of our overnight stay at a hotel. Like a reel from a movie, the memory of that night plays over and over in my head. To this day the idiosyncratic ordeal I experienced is unexplainable, but I'll do my best to relive my extraterrestrial or spiritual communion.

Like I said earlier, I was sick, but I'm sure it wasn't a fever that caused my out of body experience. It was too real, too vivid, for it to be just a dream. I was in bed, trying to sleep, when suddenly I felt I was being transported through the clouds. I remember it being very peaceful. The next thing I can make out is lying on what looked like some kind of stainless steel, surgical bed. I was surrounded by beings that were extremely, visually bright. There was an illuminating light above me and I felt very warm and safe. It's hard to explain. All I can say is, I felt a presence of welcoming warmth. I didn't want it to end and I didn't want to leave.

I recall sitting up in bed back in the hotel room and not knowing where I was or how I got there. The oddity of it was I found myself alone in that hotel room. My family wasn't around. Where were they? I had no idea. I was dazed and confused.

Now you're probably wondering if I was miraculously healed. No, there wasn't a "laying on of hands". I don't think I was in heaven because I wasn't on my death bed and why would there be an operation table inside the pearly gates. I do believe I was taken somewhere in the universe by something not of this world. Whatever it was, it embodied pure tranquility. Maybe it was angels or maybe it was aliens. Either way, I wanted to stick around.

The road trip from a feverish hell was over and I'm back at my grandparents upstairs not wanting to take a bath because of a "Peeping Tom" ghost. Thank heavens our living quarters at their house was only temporary because our new home was close to being built. By the end of summer, dad will be leaving for Nam and I'll be attending a spanking, brand new Catholic School. Oh great! It's just what the doctor ordered; more "no nonsense" nuns. I CAN HARDLY WAIT! Yeah right, nothing could be further from the truth. Only I didn't realize the truth would eventually hit me right between the eyes.

BOOK TWO

THE TAUNTING

THE TAUNTING

A contemptuous shiver, creeps up your spine.

And its insults and scornful manner by design.

For, a future's bleak and it's difficult to go on.

When dealing with death and its fear is strong.

Open your eyes and see a spirit world unseen.

Its veil will be lifted for those believe deemed.

2023

"THERE IS NO NEED FOR WAR ANYMORE
WE'VE FOUGHT ENOUGH IN THE PAST BEFORE"

M.M.D

CHAPTER 26

Dad leaves for South East Asia to a war in Vietnam I wasn't even aware of. When you're a kid the nightly news doesn't hold a candle to watching cartoons. That soon changed with our father thrown into the mix of the chaos. My sister and I started to view the evening news with our mother religiously. We would snuggle in her bed praying for the war to end. No wonder I had plenty of nightmares. Even back then I knew how senseless it was when man vs. man equals death. Not only that, dead bodies were tallied like counting sheep. How unsympathetic that count seemed. It felt like the headlines rooted for the grim reaper to strike again!

It's scary to think that death is a depiction of the grim reaper that roams the Earth. Legend portrays it as a shadowy, skeletal figure that's shrouded in a black, hooded robe carrying a scythe that looks like a sickle to harvest human souls. The myth first appeared in Europe during the 14th century when the world's worst pandemic cursed the planet with the Black Death. Folk history believes, before the disease unfurled its havoc, ghostly figures were seen spreading a fog across the fields. They were using their scalpel weapons to unleash the mystical, fatal mist.

It's kind of like what the American government did in Vietnam to clear the thick jungles so troops could come in and out of the war zones. Forests were laid barren in order for enemy soldiers to be killed. They thought it was a win/win scenario. Little did they realize, or maybe they did, their grandiose idea would backfire and veterans to this day would be suffering from the deadly, Agent Orange used to rape the environment. My family has first-hand knowledge of the horrendous after effects from a "Rainbow Herbicide" used in a herbicidal, tactical warfare. I would think the military and powerful, high-up executives would know better that one doesn't mess with Mother Nature. If you're not careful, you're in for a rude awakening because she'll inevitably bite you in the ass!

All the while this little known secret is kept from my dad and everyone else. My twin sister and I continued watching the nightly news with our mother counting down the days until our father would come home. I'm also well aware school was about to begin. That'll put a damper on late nights with mom. Not only that, just the thought of having to deal with nuns had me on high alert. To me parochial teachers wearing a traditional, religious habit resembled those infamous hooded reapers!

"I CAN THANK MY LUCKY STARS FOR THE NIGHT THERE ARE WISHES TO BE MADE BY ITS LIGHT"

M.M.D

CHAPTER 27

School was about to begin and staying up late on a week night was about to end. The dog days of summer have stopped barking. The heliacal rising of Sirius' star system can no longer be blamed for summer's blistering, sultry days. Why because stargazers back then with ancient, Hellenistic astrology believed the alignment of the stars caused the heat, drought, violent thunderstorms, unfortunate bad luck and mad dogs. WOW! The Greeks sure did put a damper on summer by comparing it to hell. I'm thinking Grecians were probably just hot and bothered and desperately wanted their kids back in the classroom. If that's the case, I wish having to go back to school was a Greek calends; "a point or time that will not exist".

I can thank my lucky stars I didn't get a nun for an instructor. I must admit my sixth grade teacher was pretty nice and she noted and encouraged my writing. Still, it was school and that meant having a way to get there. Since our mother was not a morning person my sister and I would end up walking most days. It wasn't so bad. The long, arduous journey gave us time to think and explore our new town's surroundings especially when we noticed a certain house along the way.

The house mysteriously taunted us. Every time we'd skip passed this particular home, there was an instant, unexplained, spiritual connection. We would ask each other, "Who do you think lives there and why are we so captivated?" It was like it had a magical spell over us.

It didn't help our curiosity either when at Christmas time the quant abode was decorated to the hilt. It only enhanced our infatuation and wonderment towards the property. If only this brick edifice could speak, it surely would tell a story. I had a strange, uneasy feeling, somehow, someday, our lives would be written within its ensuing, storybook pages.

**"IT'S STRONGER THAN THE STRONGEST BOND
THAT HOLDS TOGETHER NEVER BROKEN GONE"**

M.M.D

CHAPTER 28

Not having a dad for a year was bittersweet. On one hand, we loved and missed him very much. On the other hand, he wasn't there to constantly bark orders at us or punish us if we got into some kind of mishap. So that right there was a recipe for disaster because with that wide range of freedom, accidents were bound to happen.

My brothers reminded me a lot of the explorers, Lewis and Clark. The one difference, they weren't hunting for uncharted territory. Instead, they were hunting for undiscovered old bones; fossils to be exact. With the help of construction workers building new homes in the area, the digging was already dug. It was easy pickens! All you needed to do was look down for geological gems. However, my one brother didn't get that memo about watching your step.

You see, my younger, middle brother accidently stepped into a puddle of acid that was illegally dumped on the premises. Needless to say, it was a nightmare. The skin on his foot was peeling off like a snake shedding its skin. He was rushed to the hospital. Thank goodness the third degree burns eventually healed, but it left scars physically and emotionally. Usually I trek along to find rock treasures for our petrology collection. Only this time I had an uneasy feeling about going and decided to stay home. I sometimes wonder if I had been there, maybe the accident might not have happened. Maybe I could have prevented it. When I was a child, I wish I could have used my gift of internal foresight to better interpret the future.

Even when a catastrophic situation was right before my eyes, there was nothing I could do, but watch. As kids we pretty much had free reign roaming the neighborhood while riding our bikes. Of course the ratio between the number of bikes and siblings never matched, so that meant someone always had to piggy-back behind the driver. Once again my younger, middle brother happened to be in the wrong place at the wrong time.

I was on one of the bikes. My sister and little brother were riding on the other bicycle. We were on top of the hill making sure there were no cars heading in our direction. The coast was clear. From the minute my twin started to peddle down the hilly street, I saw the crash in my mind before it even happened and there wasn't a damn thing I could do about it. She lost control, hit the curb and they both flew head over heels into the air. By the time I made it down the hill all I could do was peel them off the ground and help them home.

To this day the haunted memory plays in my head. Could it be a guardian angel fast forwarded my life's movie scenario and I was able to see my childhood adventure play out before my eyes? All I know is it might have been me lying on the turf covered with road rash. For some reason I stayed back from racing down the hill. I truly believe, with all my heart, these spiritual beings are here on Earth to protect and guide us!

"EVEN GOD NEEDED A MUCH NEEDED REST
TAKE THE TIME TO SLOW DOWN HIS REQUEST
M.M.D

CHAPTER 29

The war in Vietnam was taking a toll on the country and my family. Dad had been gone for half of his one year tour. Writing letters just didn't cut it anymore. Not even pop's writing home about a female Vietcong informant while doing his laundry found a picture of planes and soldiers that my oldest brother drew lifted our spirits. The wanna-be spy thought my brother's drawing was some kind of a secret mission and tried to pass it on to our Northern adversaries. No, not even a letter like that could cure the ache our parents felt being separated. It was time for some R&R!

The term R&R can be translated as "Rest and Relaxation". What better place than beautiful Hawaii; a romantic, island paradise! It was just what mom and dad needed. I remember our mother returning from their little rendezvous recharged for the remaining months of separation. However, to her surprise, she also came home with a bun in the oven!

I'm guessing mom and dad did some cooking over there because she soon found out she was pregnant. So let me set the scene for you. Dad had been gone for almost a year and mom was growing a belly. The term R&R now meant "Rude and Rumors". Neighbors had started to talk and what they were saying was not for virgin ears. To make matters worse, the day our dad came home from Nam was not a celebration, but a realization on how mean and ugly people and our country can be.

Back in those days most homes had party lines which meant you shared the phone with someone else. Sometimes when you picked up the receiver there would be another person on the other line. Our mother was waiting for dad's call with news he was at the airport. You can imagine how excited she was, but the person on the other end didn't care and wouldn't free up the line. Not only that, we knew who the lady was and that she knew us. Whenever mom tried to hear for a dial tone, she got an earful of dirty words saying she was a slut. Needless to say, it hurt mom very much.

Dad's homecoming was also an eye opener. We made signs welcoming our father home, but we were warned by the Army not to display them. Picking him up from the airport resembled a get away car for a villain. My dad was spit on and mocked by calling him a "Baby Killer". He had to shed his uniform in order to make it out unscathed. Not only did the citizens of the United States abandon my father, but they wanted me to feel ashamed of my dad. Let me tell you, I've had nothing but love and respect for him so the shame is on America. I just wish deceased veterans from the Vietnam War serving our country had the privilege to hear, "Thank you for your service," before they became the despised ghosts from a divisive conflict!

"BLESSINGS ARE NEVER TO BE FORSAKEN
LIKE BREATH THEY MAY ONE DAY BE TAKEN"
M.M.D

CHAPTER 30

Dad's homecoming was truly a blessing. It never dawned on me that he might have been killed over there. For some reason I just knew he would come home. Never once did I doubt it. Maybe all the prayers we prayed actually put an invisible force field of spiritual protection around him. It kept the bullets away, but unfortunately not the imperceptible side-effects of being in the military.

My father was very patriotic. It was his honor to serve his country. He didn't think twice about going to Vietnam. To him the thought of others deserting their duty felt like a thorn in his side. Back then when the draft was in effect, he felt it was wrong to avoid one's duty to serve.

I never dreamt how upset it made him until I innocently squealed on a teacher. I didn't mean to. I mentioned one night at the supper table, without giving it a second thought, about my teacher telling the class that if he was drafted he would move to Canada to avoid the war. You should have seen my father's eyes. I thought they were going to pop out of his head and you could literally see steam coming out of his ears. He was so mad he took it out on me with harsh words. If I had known, what he was planning, I gladly would have taken a beating instead.

Nothing prepared me for the aftermath of being a tattle tail. Unbeknownst to me, dad played golf with the superintendant of the school and of course, with my luck, they had a round of golf scheduled that weekend. My dad wanted to know how a wanna-be draft dodger could teach such unpatriotic garbage. It didn't help the situation when a week earlier, I had a homework survey asking to agree or disagree with the Vietnam War. I was forbidden to participate in the survey. So you see how my snitching was the straw that broke the camel's back.

My teacher was furious when he was reprimanded. I was escorted to the dreaded principle's office and was interrogated like a criminal. Of course, my teacher denied saying such things, but I heard what I heard. To make matters worse none of the other students had my back. They all claimed they didn't hear him say it. That was probably what saved him from getting fired. When we left the office to go back to the classroom, my teacher cornered me and pushed me up against the wall, I could see the anger in his eyes and could tell he wanted to kill me. He sternly whispered in my ear, "You think I'm lying, don't you?" I looked him straight in the eyes and repeated what I told them earlier. "I heard what I heard!" I didn't back down. I didn't give in to their demands that I renege on my statement. I kept my honor and told the truth. I know my classmates lied because they were afraid. I didn't have any hard feelings towards them because I totally understand why they did it. I wasn't going to let a liar win which would have me lie to myself. The funny thing was, my teacher respected me after that. Believe me, it takes courage to stand up for righteousness when they think you're a perjurer.

"COURAGE COMES FROM YOUR HEART
THE MIND THINKS SO YOU WON'T START"

M.M.D

CHAPTER 31

It takes courage to open up about oneself when there's a good chance you'll be ridiculed. I know from experience how belittled you're made to feel, especially when it's about the supernatural. People look at you like your some kind of weirdo, but not everything we hear or see can be explained. Take for example my grandfather who had a first-hand encounter with a ghost. He swore he was visited by a spirit before his death. I for one never doubted him.

Grandpa suffered from asthma when he was younger, but miraculously overcame it to live a good life. So it wasn't a surprise when pneumonia came knocking when he was in his latter years. The illness made him weak and unable to climb the stairs to the upper bedroom. My grandparents had to move their sleeping quarters downstairs into the dining room for health reasons. It was here where the specter appeared to him.

First, I need to describe the lay-out of their home to better explain the apparition's flight path. The kitchen, dining room, living room and stair landing was like one big circle. There were no doors to stop you from continuing to the next room. I'm guessing it wouldn't matter anyway if you were a ghost because they can go through closed doors. Nonetheless, one evening when grandpa was lying in bed a celestial being appeared levitating above him. He sat up to witness a white shadow fly throughout the house. It floated into the dining room where he was sleeping several times and then disappeared.

His spiritual phenomena took place for about a week. It wasn't long after that my grandfather passed away. Before he died, grandpa shared his thoughts about what he had seen. He knew he was close to dying and this was a sign that the end was near. He believed an angel was staying close by to take him home to the afterlife. I just remember a peaceful glow on his face when he shared this story. I wish I could tell my grandfather, "Thank you." Because of him, I have comfort knowing we are not alone when we pass through death's door.

"YOU'RE JUST A SWEET PEA INSIDE POD'S TOMB
THE DAY CONCEIVED WITHIN MOTHER'S WOMB"

M.M.D

CHAPTER 32

The stork would soon be delivering a baby boy or girl to our family. We're so excited. The crib has been assembled in our parents' bedroom overflowing with infant paraphernalia. You know, diapers, sleepers, receiving blankets, little booties, stuff like that. Strategically placed next to the baby's bed was an antique rocking chair. I'm sure mom wanted to be as close to her newborn for those middle of the night feedings. Everything seemed perfect. We couldn't wait for the day to come.

Or maybe I should say the night. It was in the early evening when the baby decided it was time to meet the fam. Dad told my sister and I we could sleep in their bed and if the baby arrived he would wake us up with the good news. We could hardly fall asleep. We were giggling and whispering about having a new sister. We were so happy. It never dawned on me it could be a boy. I just had a feeling it was a girl.

The next thing I remember was sitting up in the morning, rubbing my eyes and staring at my sister who was also awake. We both had an expression of uncertainty on our faces. Did dad wake us up in the middle of the night? Was it just a dream? No, it was a nightmare. Dad did wake us up, but in lieu of the good news we were hoping for he instead told us our new baby sister wouldn't be coming home.

They named her, Joanna Marie. Our mother wasn't allowed to hold her, or even see her because of her deformities. They thought it would be too hard on mom. Our mother was in a room with another lady and nurses kept bringing in her baby which must have been difficult for mom having to see this lady with her newborn. How insensitive and cruel that was! All the while doctors kept asking mom if she had handled any kind of toxic materials during her pregnancy. It wasn't until years later that my dad connected the dots with Vietnam and the herbicide Agent Orange to Joanna's demise. Our baby sister died ten days after her birth. Our mother died that day too. She didn't die in the literal sense, but after the death of her baby she was never the same.

"DO NOT BE AFRAID OF DEATH

IT IS LIFE WITHOUT BREATH"

M.M.D

CHAPTER 33

The loss of our baby sister felt like a nail being pounded into our hearts. Death had swooped down and snatched an innocent infant from our mother's arms. Life as we knew it had ended. We were now a grieving family and mom was drowning in sorrow. It is said that people are more likely to die when they're in mourning. It's a scientific phenomenon known as the "Widowhood" effect. Only our mother was grieving from the loss of her infant, not her husband, but also the loss of herself.

Joanna was inside of her for nine months. When Joanna died so did mom. Anguish can put a heavy toll on a person's health; especially when it's distorted as in Maladaptive Grief. This occurs when an individual is unable to progress through the stages of grieving. We had no idea how deep the tentacles of lament suffering had embedded into our mother's soul.

Dad was hoping a change of scenery would help with mom's sadness. There were too many bereavement memories in our home so he decided to buy a new house. We had just gotten back from checking out the new pad and our parents picking out colors for the place. It was a school night and I decided to take a bath. My sister was helping mom with laundry in their bedroom. In the amount of time it took to bathe, hell was unleashed.

It was like I walked into a horror movie. Dad was frantically calling for an ambulance. My twin sister was sitting next to mom on the bed, trying to keep her from tumbling over. All the while, mom was mumbling some kind of gibberish and drooling from the mouth. What on Earth happened? One minute everything was starting to make sense, the next, our world once again was upside down and crumbling right before our eyes.

All I remember was staring out my brothers' bedroom window watching for the paramedics to come. Our neighbor, across the street, volunteered to help me take care of the boys, so dad and my sister could go with the ambulance. Once at the emergency room, it took a long time before mom was seen by a doctor. It didn't matter anyway. There was little they could do about her prognosis.

I knew she wasn't coming home. Even with adults saying, "Everything will be fine." I knew they were lying and trying to put on a brave face. I decided not to go to the hospital because she was in a coma and unresponsive from the stroke. I wanted my memories of her with life. Not death! She died several weeks later from brain cancer. Our dad and aunt came to our school to tell us she had passed away. I walked out of there feeling so alone and abandoned. It was as though God had forsaken us!

"IMAGINE OUR WORLD WITHOUT PAIN
IS IT WITH DEATH WE ARE TO GAIN"

M.M.D

CHAPTER 34

Imagine as a child leering at your mother as she's lying in a casket. There are no words to express the deep loneliness of being abandoned. You stare in disbelief. I wanted to scream at her, "Get up, you can't be dead!" "Who's going to take care of us?" "What's going to happen to us?" Thankfully my crying kept my thoughts to myself. So like obedient robots my sister, three brothers and I shook hands and gave hugs to family and friends giving their last respects to our mom.

I didn't want all those people there. It felt more like a circus than a sign of respect for my dead mother. I looked around the room feeling numb. Nothing they could say helped with my anguish. To tell you the truth, they shouldn't have said anything. The only solace to me was my uncle, our dad's brother, holding my hand and not saying a word. It was all I needed to hear.

To this day, I close my eyes and still see mom caressing her childhood prayer book and rosary in her dead hands. My mother said a rosary every night when she was alive. It was fitting she died on the day of the Feast of the Rosary. I know in my heart that was not coincidental. I wish I would've asked my father if I could keep my mom's little prayer book with the picture of the Virgin Mary on its front cover. Mom had a deep devotion to the Blessed Mother. It meant a lot to me. If I had the book, I'd have a loving memory of our mother to hold on to. Needless to say, I chickened out. I probably would've been scolded in front of everybody for being disrespectful. Anyway, dad was in no shape to abide to a child's whimsical wish. He was dealing with his own grief.

The day of the funeral was cold and dreary and that is how most of our relatives began to treat us. I swear they looked at us like we had some kind of plague. After the service, we were shunned like lepers as though we were cursed. Which they made perfectly clear they wanted no part of!

"LIES ARE THE DEVIL'S JOKES
HE HIDES WITHIN AND POKES"

M.M.D

CHAPTER 35

It's a funny thing about conspiracy theories, many times they are inner twined with a lie. Take for example, a few of mom's siblings believed the death of our mother was our dad's fault. They thought, "She'd be alive if they hadn't been living in Oak Ridge, the Atomic City." If that was the case, then the rest of us should be dying of cancer from radiation. I just think they needed someone to blame to mask their inconsiderate behavior towards mom when dad was in Vietnam. Not one of them visited us when dad was away. It's pretty sad when they bitched about the loss of their sister, but didn't care one iota when she was alive. How they treated her is still an open sore. It felt like a slap in the face!

We were on our own after mom passed away. At fourteen my sister and I took over the role of housekeeper, chef and child rearing. I'm not gonna paint myself as a martyr because my twin did most of the work. I can't thank her enough for all that she did. I feel bad we called her "grandma' back then, but come to think of it, she was very bossy. We were all dealing with our own demons. Hers was to keep things in order and mine was to be left alone. I didn't want to see or be with anybody. Shoot, I could barely make myself go to school. There were times when I'd hide under the bed until dad went to work. In the mornings, I'd tell my sister I wasn't feeling well so she could inform my teachers. Dad was clueless. He had no idea I was skipping school, but mom did!

One day I was trapped under the bed for what seemed like hours instead of minutes. Dad was taking his own sweet time. I just wanted to get back into bed so I could forget about my life. Finally, I heard the front door slam shut. That was my cue I could now crawl out from under my secret hiding place. I felt dead inside and all I wanted to do was sleep. I wanted to be left alone. Little, did I know, I wasn't alone. As I was making myself comfortable a presence appeared by the foot of the bed. I sat up and cried, "MOM!" It was wearing a white robe that looked just like our mother's.

The spirit had its back towards me and it slowly turned to face me. I was so happy! So I scooted closer to the edge, but whatever it was it wasn't reflecting what I was feeling. Its face expressed anger. It then slapped me and disappeared without a trace. I sat in bed crying and asking, "Why, why, why?" I can tell you right now, whatever it was, it knocked some sense into me. After that day I stopped playing hooky. I never told dad about what happened because I was afraid of getting into trouble. Besides, dad was dealing with his own troubles because fate had more tribulations in store for us.

"PAIN IS A BLESSING IN DISGUISE
BEING THANKFUL IS VERY WISE"
M.M.D

CHAPTER 36

"Naked I came from my mother's womb and naked I will depart. The Lord gave and the Lord has taken away, may the name of the Lord be praised." Job I :21

In the Bible there is a story about a man whose name was Job. This man was upright and extremely honest. He loved God very much and he shunned evil. You'd think his life would be a bed of roses. It was anything, but. He was victimized by the devil with God's blessings. Job was afflicted with painful sores from head to toe and he lost every thing. He lost everything, but his faith in God!

Can you imagine being persecuted by Satan with God's approval? I can. Not only did our family lose a baby sister and a mother, but tragedy wasn't done with us. You'd think we had suffered enough, but no, there was more misfortune yet to come.

We were pretty much on our own with no mother in the house. Dad not only had his daytime job. He also started selling insurance on the weekends. So you can imagine the freedom we had. My sister and I tried to keep the reins on our brothers, but to no avail. They were off and running with friends. Our youngest brother was riding bikes with the neighbor boy when they decided to go to the local convenient store. The only thing is, they had to cross a busy highway to get to the place. His buddy made it safely. Tragically our brother was hit by a truck. Before the ambulance arrived, they thought he was dead and laid a sheet over his body. Our brother's companion rode his bike home and told us the unthinkable news. It felt like God was punishing our family with the death of our mother, our sister and now our brother. Praise the Lord he wasn't dead. By the time our father and I made it to the emergency room, he was crying and alert. He was alive, just barely. He had a skull fracture, abrasions and a broken hip. Needless to say, he had a long stint in the hospital for recovery.

This brings me to my next despairing story. Dad was spending as much time as he could with our brother in the hospital. He thought the rest of us were safe and sound in school. It never occurred to him that I would end up in the hospital too. You see, I was playing softball in gym class. My teammate hit a line drive down the middle and I being on third booked it home. The catcher was hogging the plate, so I ran into her hoping she would drop the ball. She dropped the ball alright, but I also broke my wrist. The principal couldn't get a hold of pops because he was visiting his son in the same hospital that my aunt ended up having to take me to have my arm placed in a cast. Dad was going back and forth from my brother's room to check on me in the emergency room. I can't imagine the deep despair he was feeling.

That is why my sister, when the results came back positive from the TB test at school, begged them not to tell our father. She knew it would be the straw that would break the camel's back. They agreed to let her walk to the County Health Department to get her medicine each month. Thankfully, dad never found out about her bout with tuberculosis. It was by the grace of God we made it through those tumultuous times and just like the story of Job, there's a happy ending!

"IN-BETWEEN BLACK AND WHITE
MAYBE GRAY THE RIGHT BRIGHT"
M.M.D

CHAPTER 37

It's kind of funny that dad's dating situation reminded me of the fairytale, "Goldilocks and the Three Bears". I remember one of dad's girlfriends being too cold. She was a vegetarian and for Thanksgiving she made a tofu turkey. "YUK," not quite the traditional homemaker. One other girlfriend was too hot. She was a free spirit and drove a sport's car; not quite the motherly type. What dad needed was to find someone just right for his five kids.

I truly believe it was his mission to find us a new mom and I believe in my heart our mother was trying to help him. There was a pizza place close to where we lived and dad would go there, every so often, for a much needed break from reality. He began to notice a waitress and he asked her out on a date. Their relationship kicked off immediately. I'll say! They were engaged within a week of seeing each other. Not only that, our new mother to be lived in the house my sister and I took notice of when walking to school. It was like she was predestined to be apart of our lives and we sensed it years ago.

You can imagine how mom's family felt, especially when they thought dad's fiancee looked a lot like his deceased wife. You would think our relatives would be happy for him. It was just one more reason to avoid us. The shoe was on the other foot when on their wedding day it was a private affair and most family and friends were not invited. I'm sure they imagined they were being shunned. It wasn't that at all. They were married on Thanksgiving Day and decided to make it a small and simple celebration. It was about our family; in with the new out with the old.

The wedding reception was at our new mother's parents' home. Did I fail to mention our stepmother lived with her parents? So the taunting house, that we used to walk by, was not hers. Not only that, her birthmother had passed away when she was a child and our step grandmother was our new mom's stepmother. Like the story of "Cinderella" our new mother was sometimes treated badly by her evil stepmother. It was as though the house was trying to tell my sister and I, "Help her!" You could feel the dark energy lurking within its walls, especially upstairs in our stepmom's bedroom!

"THE COSMOS IS BUT A MYSTERY
FROM PAST AND TODAY'S HISTORY"
M.M.D

CHAPTER 38

There are no words to explain the uneasy feeling I got when entering our new mom's old, upstairs bedroom. The only way to describe it is like trying to walk in a cosmos mystery area. Your equilibrium is completely off balance, like having vertigo, and that's how it felt when we stepped through the bedroom doorway into another dimension.

The room seemed normal enough as we helped mom gather her things to take to our house; her new home. But I could swear there were eyes staring at us and watching our every move. You're probably thinking it's just a child's imagination going wild. NOPE! We all had goose bumps as we experienced the same eeriness that something wasn't quite right here.

Through the years, I have kept my distance from that room. My other siblings, especially my youngest brother, were not so lucky. One time he was visiting and spent the night upstairs in mom's forsaken bedroom. At the witching hour he woke up to find himself levitating over the bed. Was it just a dream? He swore it really happened and I believe him.

I also believe that house was filled with dark secrets. Mom's stepmother was nice enough to us, but not so nice to her step daughter. She wasn't physically abused, but you could tell she had been mentally tormented in the past. I can only imagine what she went through as a child. Just within the small amount of time we spent there, we were able to witness a snippet of her mistreatment. Take for example, her stepmother not talking to her for a whole year. Mom was basically dead to her. It takes a person that perverted to ill-treat someone they supposedly love. I'm sure mom wanted to get as far away from her stepmom's insanity as possible. Maybe that is why she said, "YES!" to our father's proposal for marriage within a week of dating. Come to think of it, they both had their reasons to move out of state; hoping to escape their tormented lives.

"I HAVE BUT ONE MOTHER AT BIRTH
EVEN WHEN SHE'S TAKEN FROM EARTH"

M.M.D

CHAPTER 39

We were officially a family. So to make it truly official, dad and our stepmother decided she should adopt us. They wanted to make sure if anything happened to our father, our stepmother would be able to raise us. It sounded good on paper, but we as kids were never able to read the fine print.

I would never have agreed to be adopted knowing our birthmother would be deleted from our birth certificates. It wasn't until years later that my siblings and I discovered the truth. Our mom was not only dead, but erased from being our birthmother. The state of Kentucky was actually declaring our stepmother as our birthmother and totally deleting our real mother.

My deceased, real mom is always with me. There's not a day that goes by I don't think about her. So she was on my mind the day of our big move to South Dakota. Dad was hoping to leave all those heart wrenching memories behind. He wanted to start anew with a new wife, new city, new job, new house. It was like he was trying to erase her memory. Little did he realize, all those living memories, are imbedded in one's soul. They're stored in a memory bank. Ready or not someday life will make withdraw.

Our new home had no memorabilia of our mother. Dad pretty much got rid of any kind of remembrance of her. Luckily, my sister and I were able to stash away some nick-knacks she treasured and are now treasures of ours. Later on we were able to go through some old family photos that were hidden from us for years. To this day, I don't know why. Maybe it was just too painful for dad and he thought it was the same for us. If only he knew that the real pain was not being able to keep her memory alive. There were many times at night I would cry myself to sleep, trying to remember what my mother looked like. I was afraid if I couldn't remember, I might lose her forever.

Anyway, I must admit, I was really glad we moved to a completely different state. It was like getting the stink blown off you. Moving was a chance to start fresh and with that dynamic anything was possible!

"HOPE IS A GIFT FROM THE HEART
A WISH IS GRANTED NOT TO DEPART"

M.M.D

CHAPTER 40

I was hoping that attending a brand, new school in a completely different state was the fresh start I needed to become something I didn't want to be; shy. I was totally thrown for a loop when my old alma mater was dwarfed in size compared to my new high school resulting in me becoming more withdrawn and isolated. I must have looked like an easy target because I was searching for any kind of friendship. It never dawned on me that my search for fellowship would make me a perfect subject for psychological manipulation.

Some say a cult is an organized, small clan of people having religious beliefs or practices regarded by others as strange or sinister. The purpose of a cult is to dominate its members by an unorthodox or spurious leader. I had no idea. It seemed harmful enough when I was lured by a classmate into a red brick building next to my school. The person who greeted us was friendly, a little too friendly, and right away I sensed something wasn't kosher. Hindsight, I should have known something was up instead of letting my guard down.

I was led into the main living quarters and asked to sit down on a dingy couch. The room was brightly lit by the sun's rays shining through the windows, but I could also feel a darkness. Even though I was left alone I knew I wasn't alone. I could hear whispering voices in the walls telling me to get the heck out of there. Before I could make my escape a group of brainwashed zealots wearing black hooded robes appeared. They were holding hands and chanting what sounded like gibberish. The girl who invited me tried to take my hand to join in. It was a wake up call for me. I was desperate for a friend, but not that desperate. Was it a witches' coven? I didn't stick around to find out. I ran out of there as fast as I could. To tell you the truth, I wasn't sure if they'd let me leave. I was invited in confidence to their weird ritual and I'm guessing they didn't want it exposed. Dutifully, my so called friend warned me not to mention it to anyone. For some reason I had an uneasy feeling that if I did, something nefarious would happen to me. So mum was the word.

I kept my silence and after that I became more skeptical when making friends. The only time I truly came out of my shell was when I was dancing. When I'm cutting a rug, I magically transform from an introvert to an extra extrovert. The music takes over my body and I dance like no one is watching!

"I DANCE AS IF NO ONE IS THERE
WHEN LIFE'S A SONG WITHOUT A CARE"
M.M.D

CHAPTER 41

I honestly believe when I am dancing I am no longer in the physical world, but in a spiritual realm. The only way I can describe the feeling when I dance is comparing it to a Native American Ghost Dance. Leaders of certain Paiute Tribes waved eagle-wings in front of the ghost dancers' faces putting them in a trance. The dancers would then be transported to the afterworld where departed relatives were seen living the old-time, happy life.

When I'm dancing I don't need eagle feathers to put me in a trance. All I need is the beat of the music and I am in another dimension. There were times when I've danced all night at a nightclub and I've said to myself, "I could die now. I have reached nirvana on Earth." I felt that much at peace.

When my sister and I were younger we loved to go to rock concerts and to this day we still do! As soon as the band started to play I'd be out on that arena floor getting down. There were many times when I'd have concert goers watching me instead of the rock star line-up. And of course my twin would be among the circle of spectators. Afterwards she would tell me that some of the onlookers wanted to know what I was on. She would tell them, 'Nothing just the music!" They couldn't believe I wasn't high on something. It's funny because little did they know I actually was high on dancing.

That's the power music possesses. Even King David while dancing in the streets found himself leaping with joy. It is impossible not to be happy when dancing. It is a gift of pure enjoyment. When the time comes and my life on Earth has ended. I pray there will be music and dancing in heaven. And I for one will be dancing as if no one is watching!

"THE ONLY BOSS TO YOURSELF IS YOU
NO ONE ELSE MAKES DECISIONS TO DO"

M.M.D

CHAPTER 42

It's a given, if your parents own a grocery store there's no doubt you'll be free labor. Well, that was the case when my siblings and I started to work there. Eventually, we were paid for our services and I actually ended up running the produce department. For a teenager that was unprecedented. I was my own boss. I had total freedom when it came to my work schedule. As long as I got the job done, I was able to come and go without having to clock in like the other employees. It was a pretty sweet deal!

Until a certain customer started to make his presence known by his good looks, endearing demeanor and the happiest smile I had ever seen. I nicknamed him Smiley! However, I never knew when he would show up. So, I started to work more hours hoping he would come in so we could chit-chat. I had a feeling he liked me, but he never asked me out.

One night when I was at a local disco club, he asked me to dance. I was on cloud nine. I couldn't believe I was dancing with Smiley. It was a dream, come true. I felt like Cinderella! Only in this fairytale, I didn't know I wasn't suppose to end up with prince charming. At the strike of midnight, his friends wanted to split the scene and get something to eat. He asked me if I would meet them there. Oh my gosh, of course I said, "YES!"

I was stopped from going out the door by a hand on my shoulder and a voice telling me I couldn't leave. A young man, out of the blue begged me to dance with him, "just one dance." Well, this one dance ended up being many times because his friends ended up dancing with me too. By the time I got to the restaurant, Smiley was long gone. I was devastated and deeply sorrowful for what I had done to him. We never did hook up again. I had lost my prince forever because of my all consuming passion for dancing. That is what I thought and believed until one magical night!

"FATE IS WHAT YOU MAKE OF IT
BY LIVING YOUR LIFE TAKING IT"
M.M.D

CHAPTER 43

Do you believe in fate? I certainly do! The word is defined in the English dictionary as "The development of events beyond a person's control, regarded as determined by a supernatural power." In Greek and Roman Mythology, there are three goddesses, Clotho, Lachesis and Atropos. The legend proclaims they preside over the birth and life of every human. It is believed mankind's destiny is compared to a thread that is spun, measured and cut by these three, mystical Fates. Is it possible, something supernatural kept me from leaving that dance club? I'm guessing my future was already determined and Smiley was definitely not in it, but somebody else was!

By now you've gotten the idea that I love to dance, so when my cousin from our old stomping grounds of Kentucky comes to visit, there is no question what we are going to do. Of course, we have to go dancing and with the help of some college girl friends we're good to go. As you guessed, he is the only male sitting at the table with a bunch of females. Did I say sitting? Not a chance. I got him out on the dance floor quicker than you can say, "Disco!" We were dancing the night away. I literally can dance all night long; without stopping. Just because I can, doesn't mean he can. He's begging me to take a much needed break. Reluctantly, I agree.

Unbeknownst to me, while we were dancing, there was a certain fellow watching my every move. As soon as we sat down, this good-looking guy asked if I would dance with him. Immediately, my cousin jumped up and cried, "Please take her!" You see, this "cut in" intruder was not sure if I was dancing with a boyfriend, but figured his chances were pretty good that I would dance with him because of all the girls sitting at the table. My cousin was relieved to have him take me off his hands and I was thrilled to get back on the dance floor.

Did I mention he was good-looking? As soon as he held me close and we faced each other, I felt like I was hit by a lightening bolt. I was captivated by his beautiful, blue eyes and his gorgeous smile. Having a mustache didn't hurt either. At that exact moment, I knew in my heart I was going to marry this man. I even said to myself, "I'm going to marry him!" It was a feeling I can't explain and to this day we are still dancing!

"THE GREATEST GIFT A CHILD KNOWS
IS THE GREATEST GIFT A CHILD GROWS"

M.M.D

CHAPTER 44

Like my mother before me and her mother before her, I was overjoyed with the news I was pregnant with our first child. What made it even more exciting was the possibility that I could be carrying twins. My mother had my sister and I and her mother had two sets of twin boys, but the odds were not in my favor!

I gave birth to a beautiful, baby girl. My husband and I were thrilled and also a little overwhelmed as most new parents usually are. But in my case, I was a bit more anxious and feared for the life of my child. You see, my grandmother lost three out of the four boys in childbirth and my mother lost my baby sister ten days after her birth. I was afraid there was a family curse that would take my baby from me. The taunting thought haunted me.

In ancient Jewish lore there is a demonic figure known as Lilith. Her name is gleaned from an Akkadian word Lilu meaning "night monster" from the Night/Storm Demons. She is depicted as the mother of Adam's demonic offspring, Incubi and Succubus, following his separation from, Eve, his first wife. It was believed, Eve was crafted from Adam's rib, but Lilith was made from the same soil as Adam.

Lilith, refused to be subservient to him so she left her husband, Adam. Three angels tried in vain to force her back, but alas, Lilith, chose to roam the Earth forever; never to die as the first vampire.

The myth portrays the wickedness she possesses threatens the life of women in labor and their precious newborns. The only way to counteract her possession is by wearing an amulet. For the longest time, I pinned a miraculous medal in my daughter's crib, praying to keep the demons away. You may think I'm being silly, but I know there is a battle between good and evil. Insidious forces are all around us. In some cases, they're right before our eyes not far from home.

"WHERE THE SIDEWALK ENDS
THAT IS WHERE FEAR BEGINS"
M.M.D

CHAPTER 45

My parents made the big move to Colorado. So of course, we had to go visit them; especially when we received a picture of our stepmother sunbathing in the winter. How could that be? One can only imagine our astonishment because at that time we were living in the blizzard bowels of South Dakota. It was a conundrum I definitely wanted to check out. I soon discovered it was a hit or miss being able to lie out in the sun during the colder months of Colorado. Just the idea that there was a possibility made the state even more intriguing.

I also discovered, from our trips to Colorado, that something wasn't quite right at my parents' new residence. Don't get me wrong, their place was a beautiful, three level house, but still something was amiss. I could sense it the very first time we visited. My sister was giving me a tour of the home when lo and behold, as we made our way to the basement, I felt an evil presence; a profound wickedness in the room my twin sister and her husband were staying in.

A possession from a demon or a spirit; especially an evil one, has the power to take over someone's actions. It may also manifest its evil within a place, an object or an animal. At that time, my brother-in-law was heavy into drugs. Not only drugs, but airplane glue. A perfect scenario for a demonic catalyst to take over my sister's spouse and make its presence known. You could see it in his eyes that something other than himself had taken residency within his body. That is why he stayed away from family gatherings. He pretty much kept to himself and didn't say much. He thought he was being clever in hiding his addiction. The scary thing was, I know he knew we knew, what was happening to him, but he didn't care because he had made an unholy, nefarious alliance with the devil.

"DO NOT BE DECEIVED BY A DECEPTION
THE DEVIL WILL HIDE HIS PERCEPTION"
M.M.D

CHAPTER 46

The devil is the personification of pure evil. It is portrayed as a hostile destructive entity in various cultures and religions. In the three major Abrahamic religions (Judaism, Islam and Christianity) the devil is an adversary of God. A fallen angel whose pride has tried in vain to usurp the position of the one and only supreme being. The word devil in the antiquity Greek text, diabolos, means slanderer or the accuser, but the word devil is also known around the world as Satan. In Christianity, Satan is referred to as the "Prince of Devils or Evil" and has also acquired such names as Beelzebub (Lord of Flies or Lord of Dung). It has also taken on the title of Lucifer, the fallen angel of light.

Christians believe the devil's one true mission is to persuade humans to reject a virtuous life of redemption and to accept the tortuous death of destruction. Hell is a location or a dimension in which evil souls are tortured in the afterlife for their sins. It is a place referred to as the Lake of Fire. Where the dead weep and gnash their teeth because of their eternal suffering within hell's darkness of bleakness.

I sensed something demonic was lurking in our parents' basement bedroom. It was the perfect, secluded hideaway for a demon creature.

The room had no windows, so it was always dark as the night. and the temperature in that area seemed to be much colder; especially in the winter. It was an insidious incubator for nightmares. I can remember sleeping in that room and waking up from a dream that would scare the living daylights out of me. It was as though I was paralyzed and I was being held down. Those nightmares were repeatedly of a demonic nature. I never wanted to be unaccompanied down there, mostly during the night, but sometimes it was unavoidable and I would find myself in that taunting room, alone, or was I?

"TEMPTATION CAME FROM A SNAKE
TO MOCK US TODAY DEMONS MAKE"

M.M.D

CHAPTER 47

Try and imagine a slithering bull snake living in the walls of the room you are sleeping in. It's a reptile with a reputation for stealth. So while we were sound asleep, a five foot creature was on the creep. I get the heebie-jeebies just thinking about it. This thing was hunting for mice in the basement at the same time we were in bed. Did I fail to mention, demons will take possession of animals? What is a more perfect specimen than a snake?

The snake is referred to in the Bible as the evil one. It is the beast that tempted the matriarch of humanity, Eve, to eat the forbidden fruit in the Garden of Eden. I can't, for the life of me, visualize a talking snake, but I can envision a mocking spirit. Why, because my twin sister experienced exactly that.

My twin and her husband were having marital problems. His drug use was getting out of control. He usually stayed out late or never came home at all. One night when both of them were supposed to be sleeping in the basement bedroom, she started to cry while all alone. Through her tears she thought about our deceased mother and began to pray and say, "Oh mom, Oh mom!" The closet door had been mindlessly left open. To her horror, she witnessed a demonic face, within that portal, mimicking her very own words, "Oh mom, Oh mom!" She recalls the apparition to be demonically hideous and quickly ran out of the room.

Soon after my sister's terrifying encounter, our parents discovered the slinky trespasser's secret hiding place. They had plumbing work done on the downstairs bedroom inside wall and the workers, without thinking twice, asked if mom and dad wanted them to keep the snake there or to have them remove it. Of course our parents said to get rid of it. On second thought, they weren't too sure of their decision. Living out in the prairie conjured up a lot of mice. It was nice having a built in mouse catcher. But rodents weren't the only thing going up and down throughout the house. My oldest brother, from first hand experience, knew perfectly well what that felt like!

**"A NIGHTMARE IS A DREAM WITH A FRIGHT
THAT COMES OUT TO HAUNT ONE AT NIGHT"**

M.M.D

CHAPTER 48

As you can see, I wasn't the only one experiencing unexplainable, nightmarish phenomena in that downstairs bedroom. Just like me, my other siblings were also not immune to "The Twilight Zone". The eldest of my three brothers, tells a story that still taunts him to this day about such an eerie encounter in that room.

My parents' home was like a vacation retreat. There was a continual revolving door with children and grandchildren visiting during the holidays and summer months. During such an occasion, my brother got the short end of the stick and ended up having to sleep in the basement bedroom. As expected, he didn't get much sleep!

He recalls being in bed and waking up from a devilish nightmare. He quickly gets up and uses the wall as a guide to find the light switch because the room was completely dark. Stumbling he found the switch, but to his horror the lights wouldn't turn on. He searches for the door handle trying to make his escape and then runs upstairs, only to find himself back in bed. Once again, he gets out of bed and uses the wall to get to the door and he runs up the stairs to find himself back in bed just like before. This scenario goes on several more times. Finally, when he makes his way upstairs he is, thankfully, not transported back into bed after four attempts. He determines there was no way he was going to stay in that bedroom, so he slept on the living room couch.

You're probably thinking he was just sleepwalking. He maintains it wasn't anything like that. All the while this was happening he was pinching himself; making sure it was real and not a dream. It's crystal clear a dark force had manifested in that room and no one was safe from its vile claws. We were living with the dead and anyone who dared to sleep in that room felt its presence.

"IF YOU TAKE THE DARE
TAKE THE DARE BUT BEWARE"
M.M.D

CHAPTER 49

The paranormal activity, happening within the bedroom downstairs, became a family contest on who could spend the entire night without getting scared out of their wits. The middle child of my three brothers took up the challenge. You've got to understand that my brothers thrive on an adrenalin rush. One of their favorite games was whipping each others butts, buck naked, with a tightly wrapped towel to see which one fell to their knees first. Yes, I know, I have a weird family, but it keeps us in stitches. Anyway, back to the story with my brother taking the Double Dog Dare.

The room was pitched black. I mean it is so dark you can't even see your hand in front of your face. A demon could be literally right next to you and you wouldn't even know it. How scary is that to think they can be that close! Your only defense, knowing there is nothing in this world that can stand between you and a hell bound creature, but the power of prayer.

My brother was in bed trying to fall asleep. When suddenly he heard a demonic whisper in his ear and felt its cold breath on his face. The disembodied voice chanted, "PRAY!" It was as though the entity was taunting and mocking him saying, "You better start running for your life and praying I don't catch you!" Talk about a shocker. He didn't need to be told twice and was out of there.

There was one occasion when my oldest brother came home early from his college classes and discovered our sister's husband standing at the top of the stairs. As he was approaching him, my brother greeted him by name and said, "Hello!" His brother-in-law acted as though he didn't even recognize him and just stared into space with a sinister, evil look on his face. My brother quickly turned around and without hesitating left the house. He wasn't about to confront whatever this thing was that possessed his in-law. We were all afraid of what he might do, but none of us in our wildest dreams ever thought it might happen!

**"THE ONLY POSSESSIONS ONE SHOULD KEEP
ARE THOSE OF THE HEART A DEVIL'S WEEP"**

M.M.D

CHAPTER 50

In the Bible there are examples of people being possessed by evil spirits. They were captive by demons that caused an array of physical ailments such as the inability to speak, epileptic seizures, paralyses and blindness. There were also individuals spiritually transformed to do evil. My sister's husband was influenced or controlled by something not of this world, but the underworld to do exactly that.

A nightmare is a frightful dream that usually occurs during REM sleep. It can be attributed to someone having a bad experience during the day. A nightmare is also thought to be an evil spirit oppressing people in their sleep. If we stepped it up a notch; a night terror trumps it all. Night terrors are episodes of screaming, intense trepidation and flailing while asleep. There is nothing more shocking than witnessing this form of fear, especially when it's your child. Our oldest daughter woke up many times from these night terrors when we stayed at my parents' home. I felt helpless because there wasn't much I could do except try and comfort her through the horror. The funny thing was, it seemed to only occur when she was sleeping in their house.

I never experienced any night terrors, but I did wake up many-a-night in my parents' home with an awful feeling that something bad was about to happen. It was years later, after my sister and her husband separated, that my twin confided in me about her husband telling her he heard voices directing him to kill us in our sleep. She never said anything because she couldn't believe he was capable of doing such a heinous crime. He might not be able to, but the evil that possessed him was more than capable to make him commit such a wicked, evil act. Thank goodness she left him and made a fresh start in life; free from his addictions. It was about the same time my husband and I decided to move to Colorado to be closer to family. Lucky for us, my sister's ex was no longer in our lives, but I can't say that about the supernatural!

BOOK THREE
THE HAUNTING

THE HAUNTING

A frightful, tingling shiver creeps up your spine.

When, witnessing a scary apparition by a design.

For it is difficult to ignore or forget such a sight.

To be living with the dead can conjure up fright.

As the supernatural can sense when there is fear.

Within the dark of night, but the daylight is near.

2023

"SHADOWS DISAPPEAR WHERE SILENCE CREAKS
WANDERERS MOVE WITHIN THE WALLS TO CREEP"

M.M.D

CHAPTER 51

A haunted house, also known as spook house or ghost house, is believed to be inhabited by disembodied spirits of the deceased that most likely came to their demise by a violent or tragic death; such as a murder or a suicide. Lost souls that dwell within these premises are probably former residents exhibiting a deep connection with the property. For some unknown reason, they just can't let go. So when the living enter their domain, we become the intruders.

My husband and I had purchased a quaint, cut sandstone, Victorian home in the center of the city. At first glance it had the aura of a small, gothic castle with a stone edifice that looms atop a basalt bluff in fifteenth century Scotland. But in reality, it was just a creepy, old, historical house built in 1895. Still it had a lot of personality and a lot of potential. At the time, we had no clue what we were getting into. To us it was the perfect place to raise a family.

Before the big move, I would drive around the area and check on the house. I wanted to get familiar with the neighborhood and its surroundings. I must admit I was a little disheartened because the homes were built so close to each other. It did help, though, having a city park across the street where the kids could run and play. I'd then stop in front of the house and stare into its windows. I wanted to get a feel for it. I swear it felt like the house was looking right back at me. There was something unnatural in the attic, like a snide presence staring out the window. It was as though it wanted to get a feel for me. It was at that moment I began to think this wasn't going to be your, typical, run-of-the-mill house, but instead something out of the ordinary.

Little by little I started to move in household items. I'd pack the car with what I could and then make a trip to unload. One time when I was in the house by myself, I heard the front doorbell ring. I went to the door thinking it was a neighbor, but no one was there. Then immediately the back doorbell rang. I went to the back door and again no one was there. This went on several times. Each time no one would be there. Now I know kids like to play pranks and do that kind of thing, but this was during the day when children should be in school. I don't think an adult would commit such a childish act. It felt like the house was playing a trick on me. It wanted to see how far it could push my buttons. I had no idea we would soon be residing with ghosts that weren't too keen on having living and breathing roommates.

"FIRE IS THE LIGHT THE DEVIL GIVES
FOR DEATH IS THE ONE THAT LIVES"
M.M.D

CHAPTER 52

It was getting closer and closer to actually moving in. I was still bringing things to the house every chance I could to lighten the load. On one occasion I had brought some kitchen items and placed a wicker basket on top of the electric stove. I thought nothing of it because I made sure the burners were turned off. I began to arrange the pots and pans, dishes and glassware in the cabinets then locked up and left.

The next morning when I made another run I walked into the house and smelt something burning. The closer I got to the kitchen the smell of smoke became stronger. I couldn't believe my eyes when I saw the wicker basket starting to burn that I had placed on the oven the day before. Much to my surprise, every burner was turned on high, when I knew for sure every control knob was turned off. I quickly put the smoldering basket in the sink and drenched it with water. How on Earth could this possibly have happened? At the time I was the only one going in and out of the house.

It all made sense when I went down to the basement and discovered what looked like a dungeon from the dark ages; a perfect place for mid-evil torture. Also, at the bottom of the rickety, wooden stairs was a deep, round hole; an abyss with no rhyme or reason. Was it a portal to the dark and cryptic underworld? So of course we didn't take any chances, we made darn sure the concrete pit was well covered so no small child could fall into it. What really captured our attention was the subfloor found directly under the kitchen that you could see from the unfinished ceiling of the basement. The 2x8 charred, wood floor revealed a fire from the past. I'm thinking whatever kind of presence was in our home wanted to start another fire to get us out. It wanted me to know, in no uncertain terms, who was the true owner of the house. I must admit, I was a little shaken and taken by surprise by the whole, spooky, wicker basket incident, but I wasn't about to let any kind of an apparition see how much it truly scared me. I kept my cool and went about my business as though nothing had ever happened. In the meantime, I didn't divulge to the rest of the family the revelation of the supernatural haunting. Oh, but they'll soon find out!

"HOME IS WHERE THE HEART GIVES
FOR IT'S WHERE THE FAMILY LIVES"
M.M.D

CHAPTER 53

Welcome home! We had finally moved in. We were officially living in our historical house. Everything seemed to be in order and nothing felt out of the ordinary; at least in the beginning. Maybe our invisible companions wanted us to get comfortable and situated before springing any ghostly surprises on the family. Instead of letting the black cat out of the bag, all at once, it started out with small increments of paranormal activity.

Our home consisted of a freaky, unfinished basement, a first floor, a second floor where all the family slept, and a creepy, old attic. Our daughters shared a room, our son had his own room and my husband and I were across the hall. The staircase leading up to the bedrooms displayed a beautiful, stained wood banister that decorated and protected the stairway. It was the first thing you would see when entering into the foyer. It was a sight to behold!

It was also a sight to be heard. In the middle of the night, there was nothing more spine-chilling than hearing footsteps walking up the stairs when the household was sound asleep. There were, many a night I'd poke my husband to wake up so he could check on the house because I heard something. The funny thing was, he never experienced any strange phenomena. It was like he was immune to it all. However, it wasn't the case for me and the children. They too heard the hair-raising footsteps in the heart of the night. Our son, who had a bedroom to himself, slept many nights in his sisters' room on the floor because he was scared to death of what he was hearing. All three of our children experienced the phantom footsteps creeping up the stairs.

I also witnessed black shadows upstairs during the day. They would appear in the corner of my eye for just an instant and then vanish without a trace. The hairs on my arms would stand straight up at attention. There were times I thought I was going crazy because of what I was experiencing, but I wasn't the only one feeling a little loony. Our kids and pets were going down that same rabbit hole!

"ANIMALS ARE A SPIRIT'S NIGHTMARE
THEY CAN DETECT THOSE THAT SCARE"

M.M.D

CHAPTER 54

Not only are my three children going down the paranormal rabbit hole, but our poodle named, Copper, nicknamed, Copperhead; after a venomous snake notorious for biting just like him, was eerily sensing something out of the ordinary upstairs. He would cowl, shiver and put his docked tail between his legs whenever we tried to carry him into our daughters' bedroom. He'd be stiff as a board because he didn't want to go in their room. You could tell something was scaring him.

Dogs' senses are much sharper than their human owners. They can actually sense something we can't. Although a dog's vision isn't as crystal clear as you and I, their peripheral vision is much sharper. They can see out of the corner of their eye while they are looking straight ahead. So they can easily detect the presence of a dark shadow.

Dogs also have a keen sense of hearing. They can pick up noises that we ignore. This is especially true if the sound has a higher frequency level. Canines can hear voices much like an EVP (Electronic Voice Phenomenon) device. Many ghost hunters use this tool to capture evidence that the dead are communicating from the grave; much like a telephone.

Children are also susceptible to the presence of the afterlife. They have a much greater awareness of the spiritual world than most adults do. A child is the essence of pure energy and that is why children can pick up on ghostly events and paranormal energies that go unnoticed by a vast majority of grown-ups. A disembodied spirit, like a poltergeist, will cling to a living subject; most commonly a preteen girl. At the time of the haunting that was the exact age of our two daughters. The word poltergeist comes from the German translation meaning "mischievous" or "noisy spirit". The term itself goes back centuries. The vexatious spirit is known to throw things, make sounds, arrange furniture and smash glass. Their presence have also been attributed to scratching and harming those who, in some cases, are unaware they are sharing a house with these annoying spirits. But that wasn't the case in our situation. We knew perfectly well, "THEY'RE HERE!"

"BLAME THOSE THAT DON'T CARE
THEY'LL NEVER TELL YOU BEWARE"
M.M.D

CHAPTER 55

I don't blame our dog, Copper, for not wanting to go into our daughters' bedroom. As soon as one entered into the room's gateway threshold, your presence unlocked an unseen key to an unknown dimension. The aura in the room felt like there could be a bugaboo in the closet or worst case scenario, under the bed. The mythological boogeyman is an amorphous, shadowy ghost that likes to hide in dark places to scare disobedient children. Its origin came about from an ancient Middle English word, "bugge" meaning, "something frightening". Maybe that is why the mythical character, the sandman, from European folklore was also being used by parents to counteract the scary story they were telling their children of the boogeyman. According to lore, the sandman would sprinkle magical sand into children's eyes to help them fall asleep with beautiful dreams instead of nightmares. I can tell you from first hand experience this wasn't the sandman or boogeyman in our daughters' bedroom. It was something much more frightening!

How do you explain objects flying off dressers right before your eyes! I would be in their bedroom and a knick-knack would nonchalantly fall to the floor. It was as though someone came by and deliberately pushed it off. It wanted to be noticed and pretty much said, "I'M HERE!" No wonder Copper's body language was, "No way am I going in there!"

There was one incident when I was in our daughters' room standing on a stepladder cleaning their ceiling fan when the bedroom's closed door slowly opened and then gradually closed by itself. You're probably thinking a draft must have caused it, but how could that be when all the windows were shut. I swear it looked like someone opened the door and politely shut it behind them. I stood on the ladder and very calmly said, "Good Morning," and then I went about my business. It was at that moment I decided I wasn't going to be afraid anymore. It was a live and let live epiphany. I was hoping and praying they felt the same way because not all of them were on the same page. Some ghosts were nice and some not so nice. It all depended on whom or what temperament was doing the haunting; the Boogeyman or Sandman!

**"DO YOU REALLY WANT TO BE ALONE
IT IS SAFER IN NUMBERS IT'S KNOWN"**

M.M.D

CHAPTER 56

Our children were getting older, so of course our daughters wanted their own individual bedrooms. What were we to do? Well, my husband came up with the idea to move our bedroom downstairs into the playroom next to the kitchen. The upside to that equation was the room was quite spacious. The downside was we'd be sharing our sleeping quarters with the washer and dryer. Thankfully the appliances were in a closet hidden by a bi-fold closet door. I must admit, it was kind of nice being able to do the laundry while still in bed. So all in all, the move worked out for the best!

Now that our daughters had their own bedrooms, they both wanted their own separate sleepovers. Having a bunch of preteen girls spending the night wasn't my cup of tea, but for the most part the noise was kept upstairs. They usually took turns with one daughter staying at a friend's house and the other daughter entertaining friends at our house. That made it nice by not being bombarded with a bunch of high pitch, boisterous girls all at the same time. I'm sure our shadowy housemates appreciated it too!

Although, I'd have to say tolerance only went so far for ghosts and guests. It was just too tempting not to scare the pants off of a new victim. So, of course in the middle of the night there would be disembodied footsteps walking up the stairs making their way to the bedrooms. Only the bravest of friends would spend the night more than once. Our home became known as the haunted house. If only back then there would have been the worldwide fixation about the supernatural that we have today because we could have jumped on that bandwagon and made a killing. Today, I see numerous fact-finding documentaries with one sole purpose, to uncover evidence pertaining to the spiritual afterlife. Which I don't need to watch because we lived it!

"BE AFRAID TO PLAY BALL

WHEN A GHOST IS IN THE HALL"

M.M.D

CHAPTER 57

One time when a friend was spending the night with our youngest daughter, a most mysterious encounter took place. It just so happened, when the rest of the family was out for the evening our daughter and her guest had the place all to themselves. They had free reign of the upstairs so they took full advantage of the situation by going back and forth from her room to her older sister's bedroom. What could go wrong? Her sister was gone so there was nothing to be afraid of. That's what they thought!

Not only was her sister's bedroom upstairs, so was her younger brother's which they totally avoided entering. Throughout the night they were going from bedroom to bedroom using her older sister's makeup without a hitch. The only thing between the bedrooms was a short hallway allowing for just a skip and a jump from room to room and that is where the mysterious encounter took place.

While walking out of her sister's bedroom to go back into hers, to their horror, they discovered a fully inflated beach ball in the center of the hallway. How on Earth did it end up being there when that beach ball had been meticulously put away in her brother's closet by me? It couldn't have just rolled out all by itself, especially when I know for sure I had closed the closet door. Did the ghost feel left out and just wanted to join in on the fun? That pretty much put the kibosh on their fun alright. Our daughter and her friend hunkered down in her room waiting for us to come home. They were too afraid to move any where else in the house.

Realizing the effect of this experience, my husband and I eventually took advantage of this frightful paralysis by using horror movies as a babysitter. Even though our oldest daughter was old enough to watch her younger siblings, putting on a horror movie kept them on the couch until we got home. We knew that would keep them perfectly behaved and out of trouble. But when it came to dealing with the ghosts, we were downright clueless!

**"WHAT YOU SEEK MAY NOT BE IN BOOKS
JUST OPEN YOUR EYES AND TAKE A LOOK"**

M.M.D

CHAPTER 58

Living with the dead in a haunted house was not a topic one would yell from the rooftop. It wasn't acknowledged and plastered everywhere on social media like it is today. You pretty much kept it to yourself not wanting to be ostracized and thought of as being off your rocker. Even though there would be times you thought you were going crazy, it was still your little, dark secret.

I wanted to learn more about what was going on in our home so I decided to visit the library. After dropping the kids off at school and doing a few errands, I stopped by our local branch to check out a few books on ghosts and anything else I could find pertaining to the spiritual world. I wasn't surprised when I discovered my selection was limited, but I eventually found some material that I thought might help me on my ghostly journey.

At the checkout counter I handed the librarian my library card to allow me to check out the books. The lady looked at my library card and then put my I.D closer to her eyes to really study it. From the way she was acting, I thought I was in some kind of trouble. I asked if there was something wrong. She looked at me as though she had seen a ghost and said, "Is this your actual address?" I told her, "Yes!" The color of her face became a whiter shade of pale when she asked if I had the time to talk with her. Soon she was going on a break and wanted to divulge some pertinent information to me. My curiosity went through the roof, so of course I obliged.

Never in a million years would I have guessed what she was about to tell me. It turned out her grandparents lived in our house when she was a little girl and to this day she remembers it being haunted. She recalls hearing disembodied footsteps, walking thru a perfume fragrance that came out of thin air, items going missing, objects moving on their own and being terrified to go down into the basement by herself. Everything we were experiencing she was solidifying. What was truly going on in our home. It was a breath of fresh air knowing I was not going insane. We were just living with the dead in a haunted house!

"CATS AND KIDS HAVE THE ONE FINAL SAY
WITH CUTE FACES THEY GET THEIR WAY"

M.M.D

CHAPTER 59

Not only did we have human spirits living with us, but I also witnessed an animal ghost. From the time I was young I had a passion for animals. Throughout the years I've had the pleasure of sharing my life with these amazing creatures, but of all the pets I have truly loved there was one that stood out from all the rest.

Domesticated cats came from cats in the wild. It is believed they originated from the Fertile Crescent in the Neolithic Period, but the first domesticated cat on record was a cat that was buried with its owner around 9,500 years ago in Cyprus. Our cat, Mia, was half Manx with no tail of course and the other half Siamese with beautiful, characteristic markings and striking blue eyes. She was unlike any other feline I have owned. She would play hide-and-seek in the house with the kids. It was fun to watch her search for them as they called her name. Our son even took her to school for show-and-tell to demonstrate her hide-and-seek skills. He hid in the classroom and to his classmates amazement she found him. She was a very special cat and one of a kind.

So when she became sick and the vet had no clue what was wrong with her, she suddenly passed away. It took all I had to bury her in our backyard. I couldn't bear to think of her all alone, so I buried some of her treasured toys with her. She brought such joy in our lives and I wanted her to remember us in the afterlife. I kept saying to myself, "All pets go to heaven and someday we'll meet again". I didn't think that someday would be so soon.

Animal ghosts are much rarer than human spirits. They usually haunt where they lived and not so much where they died and in some cases they will linger where they felt most comfortable such as their bed or where they ate. Usually one will hear an animal ghost by it interacting with an inanimate object; such as a toy. They may even leave an imprint on where they liked to sleep like a couch or pillow. Mia's favorite place was perching herself at the turned base of the staircase going upstairs.

She appeared to me twice and then suddenly disappeared when I was heading up the stairs. Each time she looked very healthy and happy as if to say, "Don't worry about me I'm doing fine." The last time I saw her I even heard the bell she wore on her collar. I knew after that she entered into the light because of a feeling of peace that went through me. She was now in a better place. She just wanted to say, "Goodbye!" On the other hand our human ghosts were constantly reminding us they weren't going anywhere. They were here to stay!

"THERE ARE NO LUGGAGE RACKS ON A HEARSE

YOU CAN'T TAKE IT WITH YOU IS THE CURSE"

M.M.D

CHAPTER 60

The ghosts were here to stay alright. They ruled the roost by letting us know, in no uncertain terms, what's yours is also ours. Throughout the years I have collected many knickknacks and antiques. On the wall in our family's den hung a printer's tray that was once used years ago for typesetting. In that day the raised press letters were placed in the small compartments to be stored. Those compact sections made excellent little, display shelves for miniature mementos which I gladly filled.

Although, I truly enjoyed all of my little trinkets, there were some that held a special place in my heart. In the center of the hanging display I had a couple of tiny, ceramic mice that represented my children. One figure was of two young girl mice holding hands and the other was a baby, boy mouse sitting and playing with a toy. Whenever I would enter the room I'd blow a kiss towards the figures for my children. One day I noticed my tiny treasures weren't there. My little mice children were gone! My kids couldn't have taken them because the printer's box was out of their reach.

It wasn't the only thing that disappeared. I also had a pair of bronzed dice that went missing that typified my dad who enjoyed gambling in Las Vegas. Every time I'd glace at the dice I would think of him. The three items that meant the most to me out of the whole array of novelties were no where to be found. Not only that, three candlesticks from a candelabra suddenly vanished into thin air plus a carved, wooden number 21 from a homemade calendar that my father-in-law made had magically went poof without a trace. We searched and searched throughout the house, but to no avail. I think I know why they took the three, little mice and the dice; they wanted to get my attention because it meant so much to me. Why the candles and the number 21? I discovered later that if a candle flame burns blue or suddenly goes out with no apparent reason, it is a sure sign ghosts are present and want to communicate. Maybe disembodied spirits were trying to tell us to burn candles so we could have a conversation with them. And I found out the number 21 represents an angel. Were they trying to inform us we were dealing with spiritual beings? It felt like we were living in an altered reality!

"DEATH IS THE PORTAL TO THE OTHERSIDE
WHEN WE'RE THERE WE KNOW WE'VE DIED"

M.M.D

CHAPTER 61

Could it be our home was a portal for the afterlife! An unfathomable existence for life after death in which the essential part of a person's consciousness or individual identity continues to live after their physical body has died. Were we living in a parallel universe where our world coexists with the afterlife, but is undetectable because of a veil between the two dimensions; life and death? For some unknown reason that mystifying shroud was being lifted by whatever was in our house and it was gradually allowing us to see behind the hidden curtain.

One evening when the family was out and about and after returning home we noticed something very disturbing in our son's bedroom. All the pictures that were on his walls were hanging upside down. We couldn't believe our eyes. We were completely baffled and a chill went down my spine trying to comprehend how this was even possible. Who or what could have done this?

It was apparent that whatever it was had an issue with anything hanging on a wall with a frame. There were times I had gone into our bathroom upstairs and would be at the sink when artwork would fly off the wall and hit me on my backside. It doesn't make any sense that a portrait would fly off the wall and hit me when normally that picture would just slide down the wall and hit the floor. I must have been the butt of a joke when I was being targeted by an invisible bully.

One time I left a laundry basket with clean clothes upstairs in the hallway to answer the wall, home phone that was ringing downstairs. As I made it to the bottom of the stairs, the basket came out of nowhere and hit me on the back of my legs with folded clothes scattered everywhere. However I wasn't the only one getting sucker-punched from behind. On one occasion, our youngest daughter thought I tossed the basket down the stairs to hit her as a prank. Those ghosts must have had one hell of a laugh at our disquieting expense. Except I wasn't laughing and neither was anybody else!

"YOU TRY TO CONVEY TO A GUEST
A GHOST WILL BE THERE AS YOU REST"
M.M.D

CHAPTER 62

Our home was a shelter for the passions of past generations. It has stood the test of time standing as a mute witness to those that have gone before us. Its cold stones imprison the rooms and hallways of this ancient edifice only to reveal its shrouded memories to those that are perceptive to paranormal activity and sensitive enough to tune them in. Such as a good friend of my husband's that came to visit.

We were all looking forward to seeing his old classmate. Our youngest daughter was even willing to give up her bedroom so he would have a place to sleep. After dinner we were visiting on our backyard deck when the topic of our house being haunted suddenly came up. It was the highlight of the night with us telling ghost stories that really weren't just stories, but real life events. Our encounters didn't seem to bother him. He was a Special Forces, Army veteran that personified what it meant to be macho. He even rode a Harley Davidson hog on his trip across country to visit us. He reeked of machismo. Tell that to a ghost!

Well, unbeknownst to us, while he was sound asleep, he was awakened by a picture flying across the room and crashing into smithereens in the middle of the floor. The next morning when he came downstairs looking as white as a ghost, he told us what he witnessed. He said the picture flew with such force something had to have thrown it, and whatever it was, it wasn't happy he was sleeping in that bedroom. It took everything he had to stay the entire night in that room. Needless to say, he packed his bags and left that very day. He didn't want any part of our haunted house.

I guess our spooky spirit wasn't too thrilled about having a sleepover with a stranger. It pretty much wanted him out of there in no uncertain terms. I must admit, I give him kudos for staying the whole night. He said he didn't sleep a wink. You could tell he wasn't lying because his face expressed real fear and a lack of shut eye. What he experienced, I wouldn't wish on anybody. But the thing is, we couldn't just pick up and leave like our friend because this was our home and what he encountered was already a part of our lives.

**"ADMIRING YOUR CHILDREN AT YOUR FEET
WITH TRUSTING ARMS THEY REACH TO GREET"**

M.M.D

CHAPTER 63

A child can become a ghost if they were traumatized and died a vicious death. Their souls, much like an adult, sometimes do not pass on to the other side, but for some reason will remain here to interact with others that may or may not be their own family. Some ghost children are unaware they have died and are destined to roam the living world as innocent, lost spirits. While others enjoy interacting with the living and will draw attention to themselves by being playful. These children, whose lives were tragically taken from them, were not ready to let go. Their only recourse is to haunt.

I was putting folded clothes unto our oldest daughter's bed when someone pinched me hard on my side. It startled me! I grabbed my waist and turned around thinking it was one of the kids playing a mean trick on me. Looking into our son's bedroom, which was directly across the hall, I saw a little boy kneeling in front of the toy box. I yelled out our son's name, but as soon as I said it, the little boy turned around and glanced at me for a second and then disappeared right before my eyes. My jaw dropped. What did I just witness?

I wasn't the only one in our family who saw the little, disappearing boy with dark hair and black eyes. Our oldest daughter claimed she would lie in bed and see him by the toy box just as I had seen him. The small apparition seemed to enjoy playing with our son's toys. It got to the point where she would keep her bedroom door closed so she wouldn't have to see him. It is believed that children and pets are more likely to perceive ghost children than adults. I guess I can call myself "lucky" witnessing a ghost child. I just wish I was able to help this little one find his way home. But who am I to wish for anything when he thinks he's already home!

**"TO A CHILD HOW SWEET IT IS
BETTER TO RECEIVE THAN GIVE"**

M.M.D

CHAPTER 64

Halloween! It's a child's dream come true with children dressing up in scary costumes and going door to door saying, "trick or treat," for candy. Have you ever wondered how this odd tradition started? It is believed Halloween began as an ancient Celtic Festival called Samhain. It was a pagan, religious ritual celebrated on November 1st to welcome the bountiful harvest at the end of Summer. Celebrations would begin on the evening of October 31st and end at sunset the following day. The people of the village would light bonfires and dress up in various costumes to ward off ghosts they believed were walking the Earth.

It wasn't until Pope Gregory IV designated November 1st as All Saints Day to counteract the traditions of Sambain that came into play for Hallows' Eve. The evening before All Saints Day was referred to as All Hallows' Eve, better known today as Halloween which is the pagan celebration of the dead walking among the living. Later on many Christian missionaries introduced All Souls Day on November 2nd to perpetuate the idea that the dead are living among us.

From the time I can remember celebrating Halloween was one of the highlights of my childhood. To a child there's nothing better than free candy. Maybe a ghost child feels the same way. Our son after a Halloween night of frightful fun would meticulously position his bountiful stash of goodies on his desk in his bedroom with strict instructions to his two older sisters to leave his maraud treasure alone. His bag would be filled with delectable delights just waiting to be consumed by him. Soon after Halloween I would go into his room and find candy wrappers spewed all over his floor. How could this be when I checked his room in the mornings after he had gone to school? What's baffling his room would be clean before I'd go to work, but when I arrived at home before the kids got out of school, I'd find more trash. I even asked him if he somehow snuck into the house and had a candy eating frenzy. The thing of it is, he was just as upset as I was because he was missing a lot of his loot. I tried hiding the bag in his closet and various places around the house to still find candy wrappers scattered only in his room. It just became a Halloween tradition to clean up after a sweet tooth spirit!

"THEY LET YOU BELIEVE YOU'RE IN CHARGE
UNTIL THEY MESS WITH ELECTRICITY AT LARGE"

M.M.D

CHAPTER 65

The true modern American version of trick or treating comes from a German Christmas tradition of "belsnickering". Children would dress up in costumes and then go to their neighbors to see if any adults could guess their identity behind their disguises. If the children were able to trick them, they were rewarded with food and other treats. Sounds pretty much like Halloween to me.

The word "belsnickering" is rooted in the word belligerent meaning hostile and aggressive. I'm also guessing the word snickering is deep rooted somewhere in its translation meaning laughing in a half-suppressed, scornful way. And that was exactly how it seemed when we were dealing with the spirits in our home.

Our son's bedroom was becoming a hotspot for the paranormal. Not only were we visited by a ghost child playing in his toy box and who gladly helped himself to our son's Halloween candy, but we were also experiencing metaphysical activity through electrical devices in his room. One day I was sitting at his desk working on his computer, and because I am electronically challenged, my children were there to help me with my use of the apparatus. When I was done, I turned off the machine and the three of us started to leave the room. All of a sudden, to our surprise, the computer rebooted. Thinking maybe I didn't shut the computer down correctly, I had our son shut it down the second time. We thought we were good when we headed out the door, but to our horror the mechanism started to reboot again. This time we darted out the door as fast as we could. If the ghost wanted the darn thing on, who were we to argue!

We had no idea electrical devices could be used to communicate with the dead like they are today. It would have been nice to have had that kind of technology back then to speak to otherworldly inhabitants living among us. We even thought about using an Quija board, but I wasn't too keen on that idea because of our past experience when playing the game.

One night my three, younger brothers tried to conjure up the supernatural in our dungeon like basement and actually heard unusual knocking coming from within its thick, concrete walls. Little did we know, we needed to be more high tech by using an EVP; an electronic voice phenomena device. This invention is able to pick up voices of unknown spiritual origin that are not heard at the time of the tape recording, but are heard when played back. Another device used is a ghost box which is a modified radio that sweeps across AM and FM airways picking up various types of music and bits and pieces of mysterious dialogue. Unfortunately we had none of the above, but that wouldn't have stopped the haunting of our home anyway. The unsettling and unworldly phenomena made it perfectly clear it wanted us to pack our bags!

"DON'T PICK UP THE PHONE LATE AT NIGHT
FOR THE DEAD MAY BE CALLING TO FRIGHT"
M.M.D

CHAPTER 66

The concept of the paranormal using electronic technology to communicate with the living makes perfect sense when the manifestation of ghosts and spirits is a form of energy like you see in the vast spectrum of optical fibers and coextensive cables in telephone lines and televisions which is also made up of energy. Why wouldn't supernatural forces use these scientific, electromagnetic waves to travel and possibly talk to us? Life's essence is created by God and can neither be duplicated nor destroyed, but can only change its form. The living soul within us is pure energy and that energy after death never dies.

Supernatural and paranormal events had always been a topic of choice within my family. It was shared knowledge with my sister and brothers regarding the strange and unusual activity we were experiencing. The problem was, I could never produce evidence to explain the unexplained. Which made it just hearsay, but all that was about to change.

When the phone rings in the dead of night, it's a wake up call from a deep sleep, but it also alarms you that something unthinkable might have happened. Anyone who has teenagers knows exactly what I mean. So, when the phone rings at 3:00 am I'm thinking the worst. I missed the call while stumbling out of bed and trying to come to my senses. To our disbelief, the shrieking from the answering machine was not a human voice. In the midst of what sounded like eerie static was the message "GET OUT!" in the recording. The words were drawn out like a horrific song and to this day still plays in my head. My husband and I couldn't believe our ears. We were dumbfounded and extremely concerned. Whatever it was made its haunted wish perfectly clear. The only upside to its disturbing gist was that I now had solid verification we were living with the dead.

I made a copy of the wretched words "GET OUT!" on a cassette tape to prove we weren't going insane. I played the haunting message to my sister and brothers and they couldn't believe how horrifying it sounded. Each one confessed that the hairs on the back of their necks stood at attention like a warning. Since this definitely was an eye opener after hearing the telephone ring from the dead, we felt we needed the help of religious reinforcements. It was time to call in the Catholic Cavalry!

"BE NOT AFRAID

FOR THE HAND OF GOD WILL SAVE"

M.M.D

CHAPTER 67

Living with the dead had reached a pinnacle moment after being ordered to "GET OUT!" by a psycho spirit. The entity had already proven it can be dangerous. How can I ever forget the incident of the wicker basket starting to catch on fire because a pyromaniac phantom turned all the burners to high on the stove. It was time we called our parish priest because we needed a professional ghost buster!

An exorcist is a person, most likely a Catholic bishop or priest, who is granted the task to investigate cases of possible demonic possession. The exorcist is trained to cast out the devil, his demons or other supernatural beings from a person, place or an object by a religious, spiritual rite. An exorcism is the practice to evict these malevolent entities.

Exorcisms are separated into two classifications. Simple or minor forms of exorcisms is through the sacrament of baptism and RCIA; the Rite of Christian Initiation. The second type is referred to as solemn or major exorcism and can only be performed by a bishop or a priest with special permission granted by the Bishop of Rome.

This form is specifically directed to expel demons to liberate a person, a place or a possession from a demonic, devilish influence.

I'm sure our pastor didn't have special or expressed permission from the Vatican to expel demons. He offered to just bless the house. Little did we know, his blessing would be a curse. As soon as he started to climb the stairs, something behind him pushed him forward making him fall. I knew at that moment this was war. Father slowly walked through each bedroom sprinkling holy water and saying prayers to remove whatever was haunting the upstairs. I could tell by his facial expression he wanted to get the heck out of there. He didn't even make it downstairs to bless the entire house. I pretty much got the impression we were on our own. Not only did the haunting persist, but the nature of the haunting became even more brazen. It was as though we were living in a nightmare!

"HEARING VOICES IN YOUR HEAD
MAY BE TOUCHING YOU INSTEAD"
M.M.D

CHAPTER 68

The supernatural manifested into mega-supernatural after our parish priest blessed our home. It did little more than piss-off whatever was haunting our house. The nightmare was more like a waking dream with spirits blatantly becoming more defiant. There was nothing in this world that prepared me for what I was about to experience. Something unknown was about to lift the veil separating our parallel universes and I was to be its victim.

A nightmare is a frightening dream during sleep. A hypnagogic hallucination is a brief delusion that takes place as you're falling asleep; neither occur during waking hours. I know I was wide awake when I decided to lie down after seeing the kids off to school one day. It was a cold, winter morning and I just wanted to warm myself under the covers. As soon as I was snug as a bug on a rug, I noticed a hand-print pressing down on the blanket and touching my leg. It was as clear as day. It was slowly creeping up my leg and I couldn't move. It took everything I had to finally escape from the paralysis and its crepuscular possession.

All I could think of was, "What the heck just happened?" I was clearly being ghost handled. Was I in the presence of an incubus? A demon in male form that seeks to have sexual pleasure with sleeping women. Whatever it was, it made its advances in haste because I wasn't asleep. I jumped out of bed which stopped its advancements before it could go any further. Good thing because folklore has it that a union with an incubus could result in the birth of witches and demons. I must say that on some occasions my children do act like little demons, but that's another story.

That brings to mind the time I heard voices of children in the middle of the night. I was sound asleep and exactly at 3:00 am I was suddenly shaken awake because of loud talking upstairs. I was certain it was our oldest, teenage daughter sneaking in friends at the wee hours of the morning. Trying to catch them in the act, I quietly made my way upstairs. I was dumbfounded to discover that she, her sister and brother were sound asleep. Where was the noise coming from? It sounded like partying teenagers. This was definitely a wake up call. It was becoming apparent our home was a gateway for the spirit world!

"AN ORB WITHIN THE ROOM
WILL MOVE A CHAIR ASSUMED"

M.M.D

CHAPTER 69

A gateway is a spiritual threshold used as an opening to enter into the other side. Ghost orbs or spirit orbs are spherical bodies that manifest energy of light allowing them to pass through these portals. Naysayers believe that many balls of light people see are only an optical phenomenon called backscatter. It occurs when images of circular figures appear due to a photographer's flash reflecting from dust or an unfocused lens, but what if a camera's not in the picture?

It was mid-afternoon when I came home from work. I had just enough time to get myself settled before the kids got home from school. Checking to see if we received any mail, I tucked the letters under my arm and then proceeded to unlock the front door. Making my way into the foyer I noticed something out-of-the ordinary in the comer of my eye. It was a ball of light floating on the wall. Thinking it was just the sunlight's reflection, I looked around and there was none to be seen, just this one small, global object. I stared at it for awhile and it appeared to be studying me. I felt uneasy, but decided, with lack of better judgment, to go about my business and enter the dining room to open up the mail.

As I was standing at our antique dining table, I noticed the same spherical shape mysteriously floating above me on the wall. Once again I checked to see if there was some kind of explanation for what I was witnessing. While thinking there had to be a scientific reason for this, I began to rip open junk mail and unwanted bills. Suddenly, the chair I was standing next to that I had pulled out so I could have some space, started to move all by itself. I froze not believing what I was seeing. I could actually hear it slowly sliding across the carpet as though someone was pushing the chair towards the table after they had sat in it. I even bent down to see if it was really happening. It was! Not wanting to startle the entity, I politely excused myself and said, "I believe in you!" Then I calmly walked out of the house not wishing to be in the same room with the spirit and I waited for my children to come home. When they got to the bench where I was sitting they immediately sensed something was wrong because I was as pale as a ghost. After that hair-raising experience, our living with the dead turned a page to to a new chapter because we were out of there!

"WHEN THOUGHTS OF FEAR ARE RAISED
DO NOT IGNORE FOR SPIRITS WILL RAZE"
M.M.D

CHAPTER 70

I must admit it was bittersweet the day we moved from our haunted house. For thirteen years we shared our home with the paranormal. Now it was time to move on and share the love, or should I say, share the spiritual unknown with someone else. To the unexpected renter, it was an 1895, cut sandstone, Victorian house. To the ghosts, it was just another clueless victim to prey upon.

Maybe we should have warned the newest tenant about the strange activity we were experiencing, but we were never given any heads-up when we moved in, so it was like passing the hot potato on to the next player. For years we realized we were living with the dead and we dealt with it. I never, in my scariest of nightmares, dreamt it could open up a brand new can of worms for someone else who couldn't deal with it.

It was years later we came across the person who had rented our home. My husband and I, out of curiosity, asked her if she ever experienced anything unusual while living in our haunted rental. Her eyes grew as large as dinner plates and replied, "What do you mean?" We started telling her about the strange phenomena we had dealt with and how we even had our parish priest bless the house because we truly believed it was possessed. After hearing us reminisce, it was like a breath of fresh air to her. She was so thankful to finally understand and tell us her own story about the house.

Her introduction to the spirit world wasn't as apparent as ours. She said, she didn't believe in ghosts and at that time it wasn't even an option for her. She was hearing and seeing eerie things in the corner of her eye, but thought it was all in her head. It got so bad she started to see a therapist who prescribed medication for anxiety. After speaking to us, she was relieved to find out that she really wasn't going crazy. I was, once again, reminded there are revenants living among us.

Even though we've sold our historic home many years ago, sometimes I still drive by the old neighborhood just to gaze at our once ghostly house and whisper to the place, "Remember Me!" You know, it's strange, but I get a weird feeling that it actually remembers. I wonder if the present-day owners are experiencing anything unusual like we once did. And to tell you the truth, I wouldn't doubt it for a minute. And I'd even bet on it!

"IF BY CHANCE THE FUTURE IS REVEALED
THE GIFT OF PRESCIENT NOT CONCEALED"
M.M.D

CHAPTER 71

Just because we moved from a haunted house doesn't mean the essence of paranormal activity was no longer with us. It was inevitable, no matter where we end up putting down roots something strange was bound to happen. It was as though I could feel it in my bones or better yet see it in my mind.

Intuition is the immediate insight of a situation like having a "gut feeling" about present events. That is why it is often referred to as "trusting your gut". There are those who are blessed with the gift of clairvoyance. They are able to perceive things or events in the future beyond normal sensory perception. These spiritual clairvoyants can gain personal information about a person, place or an object through ESP (Extrasensory Perception). They can see into the hereafter.

I wouldn't go so far as to say that I am blessed with such a gift of clairvoyance, but I do feel that I am sensitive to spiritual energy. I can sense the emotions and auras of other people, animals and even objects. That is why I have a passion for collecting antiques. I am always on the lookout for a one-of-a-kind piece that talks to me. And it just so happened on one occasion a beautiful, cushioned, ornate, foyer bench spoke to me. Every time I'd be at this certain antique shop I'd stop and admire it. Finally, I decided to put it on lay-a-way because I felt a deep connection to it. To my horror, when I entered the store, I noticed a lady at the counter purchasing what I thought should be my piece of furniture. I was heart broken because I truly believed it wanted to go home with me. Well, a remarkable and eerie thing happened that night. I dreamt this very same antique was still at the store. The dream was so vivid I had to see for myself that it was true. I couldn't believe my eyes when I saw the beautiful bench still there. I quickly grabbed it and took it to the checkout counter. The saleswoman told me the person who purchased it brought it back because it didn't fit her decor. It must not have spoken to her like it did to me.

I've also had premonitions throughout the years like a strong feeling that something bad was about to happen. Around the time we moved from our haunted home, my husband started a house building business. At one worksite there was a very large jobsite, garbage dumpster I thought was placed too close to the street and it was going to cause an accident. The workers, including my husband, said I was being ridiculous. Sure enough, the following evening a car full of drunken teenagers lost control of the vehicle and clipped the dumpster while speeding down the hill. Luckily no one was seriously hurt, but how was I able to see the crash before it played out. I know, there are those like me, that are just more sensitive to the cosmic universe and like me, to the spiritual world around them.

"WHEN GAZING INTO THE COSMOS
A WORLD OF WONDER NO ONE KNOWS"
M.M.D

CHAPTER 72

We are not alone. Extraterrestrials have been visiting our planet since the beginning of Earth's existence, although their concept of measuring time is definitely different than our own. Maybe that is why they have an interest in our genetics and seem to be following the changes in one or two genes over a family's generational lifespan. These little, gray fellows seem to abduct certain members from the same family who they find to be amenable using those that will easily comply. If that's the case aliens may be more like us than we think; why work harder than you have to.

I have always felt a connection to anything pertaining to UFO's and extraterrestrials. It all made sense one day while I was having a conversation with my dad. We were sitting next to each other on the couch when out of the blue he said he needed to tell me something he has never told anyone else before. I held his hand not knowing what to think. He talked about being a young boy when small, gray beings would come into his room and stand by his bedside. He remembers not being able to move or scream, but having a faint memory of being taken from his bed and brought back. I wasn't prepared for what I was hearing. I told dad, "Now it all makes sense. I have also seen small beings and felt I've been taken from my room and brought back." My father, died shortly after I heard his story. It makes me happy to know I have this connection with my dad because we share an amazing, extraterrestrial legacy.

Many who believe they've been taken by aliens express the same type of traumatic, physiological reaction as those who have gone through other kind of trauma experience. The only difference is those who have been abducted are usually not taken as being serious. It usually comes down to, "Where's the evidence?" Someone can say they saw flashing lights, heard buzzing sounds, experienced a feeling of levitation, unable to move except for eye movement and saw non human figures by their bed, but without solid proof it is only hearsay.

Today, alien nanotechnology is surgically piecing together evidence to prove there really are humans being abducted. In the documentary "Patient Seventeen", a surgeon by the name of Dr. Roger Leir successfully removed an alien implant from an abduction victim. The foreign object consisted of 36 particles which is far greater than any other industrial compound. It even showed that some of the elements found in the patient could not have been made here on Earth. Are we finally getting closer to the truth about UFO's and aliens? But what if extraterrestrials decide to take a material object from a person instead of implanting one!

"MUST BE LOSING MY MIND
MY RING I CANNOT FIND"
M.M.D

CHAPTER 73

One of the best epic-fantasy novels is J.R.R. Tolkein's "The Lord of the Rings". It is set in middle-earth where a fellowship of hobbits, dwarfs, elves and men come together to destroy a ring that has the power to control the entire world. The dark lord Sauron wants to reclaim his lost kingdom and enslave everyone by controlling the one powerful ring. Throughout the story the ring takes possession of its wanna-be possessors. For example, the character Gollum referred to the ring as "my precious" or "precious". He loved and hated the ring and was tom between his lust for it and his desire to be set free from it. He finally met his doom, along with his "precious", when he seized the ring from the book's hero, but fell into the fires of the volcano at the Crack of Doom. And he and the ring were finally destroyed.

The symbol of a wedding ring is also powerful. It represents the union between two people, husband and wife, who wish to share their lives together. I never take my wedding ring off. It's as much a part of me as the color of my eyes. In fact, I've tried removing it, but it doesn't want to go over my knuckles. My ring is not going anywhere. Well, that's what I thought.

One morning I woke up to discover the gold, wedding band from my bridal, ring set was missing. The diamond ring was still on my finger, but the gold band which was below it was gone. How in the world did the gold band pass my diamond ring slip past my knuckle and come off my finger? They were both on my hand when I went to sleep. I tore the bed apart trying to find the ring. I looked on the bed and under the bed, but to no avail. I eventually went and bought the exact same gold band to replace the one taken from me. That's right, taken from me. There's no way the ring could have fallen off my finger because it took plenty of soap and water to remove the diamond ring that was still on my hand and to get both rings (including the new, gold band replacement) painfully back on.

So now every morning when I wake up I hold my breath as I make sure I have both rings on my finger. Because just like Gollum, the ring that mysteriously vanished into thin air was "precious" to me. I keep asking myself, "Who on Earth could have taken it?" I know the answer to my own question and whoever it was, wasn't from this planet.

"WHAT WAKES YOU UP AT NIGHT
IT'S THEIR RED ORBS OF LIGHT"
M.M.D

CHAPTER 74

Orbs of light, the manifestation of energy, is believed to be the paranormal power for ghosts and spirits. It is now being brought to our attention that these glowing balls of life may be the source of vitality for extraterrestrials. The United States government has kept a tightly closed-lid on the evidence for non-terrestrials, but it has come to my attention that Congress recently held its first public UFO hearing in more than 50 years.

To tell you the truth, I'm a little surprised prominent politicians are bringing up the UFO topic. As a rule our leaders don't have much to say when it comes to aliens and unidentified flying objects especially when they use the lame excuse of having to deal with all the challenges here on Earth. I think it's about time they stop treating us like children and tell us what we already know. THEY'RE HERE!

In fact the House Intelligence Committee heard from the Deputy Director of Naval Intelligence and the Undersecretary of Defense for intelligent security regarding unidentified aerial phenomena. (UAP is the new nomenclature for UFO) In their testimony they emphasized that such things are real, but it still lacks evidence for so called space invaders. What about the case where Pentagon officials claim that a "glowing red orb" once shut down nuclear weapons in Montana? Of course the government stated that technical malfunction, however rare, was the culprit. It's just another one of their weather balloons or swamp gas excuses. I'm wondering, what's my excuse?

It was late at night when I suddenly awoke from a deep sleep. I remember being awakened by something intentionally wanting my attention. Hoping I could fall back to sleep if I turned towards my husband, I wasn't prepared for what I saw in front of me. I yelled out, "Babe, what is that?" A glowing, red orb in the shape of a small, flying saucer was right before my eyes and then slowly floated through the wall. I'm sure you're thinking I was dreaming, but within the same week I woke up again to see another flashing, red orb float through the wall. To this day, I have no doubt what I saw was real. I don't care if I'm labeled a UFO conspiracy freak because I know for a fact there is too much evidence not to believe!

"THEY WALK THE EARTH OUT OF SIGHT
PARANORMAL ACTIVITY IS TO FRIGHT"

M.M.D

CHAPTER 75

Through out my life I have had a connection with the supernatural and even to this day I am traveling on a paranormal journey. To my credit I have read countless books and watched many hours of documentaries pertaining to the transcendent. But not only that, I have lived it.

I am a huge fan of the show "The Secret of Skinwalker Ranch". The name of the ranch is taken from the skin-walker of Navajo legend. A skin-walker is a baleful witch that possesses supernatural powers to transform into any type of animal or unknown cryptic creature. Supposedly the myth derived from a Navajo lore regarding vengeful shamans who cursed the Ute Tribe and their land for mistreating the Navajo Nation. And ever since then for 200 years, Utah's Uinta Basin has been cursed.

Skinwalker Ranch and the surrounding area have a reputation for being referred to as "UFO alley". (That's right up my alley) A team of scientists and experts are continually searching for logical answers concerning the numerous anomalies of strange animal mutilations, UFO or UAP sightings and the vast cases of mysterious, paranormal activity. The team uses the latest in cutting-edge technology like ground penetrating radar and drones to try and discover what is behind the secret of Skinwalker Ranch.

Our trip to Las Vegas, NV also included a stop southwest of Ballard, Utah. It was only a two hour out of the way trek from our destination to Sin City. We knew we wouldn't be allowed to go into the ranch because it is private property, but we could get pretty darn close. It was I :30 in the morning when we reached the intimidating, stop sign letting us know we better not go any further. So we didn't. Of course we got out of the car to take pictures and video proving we actually were at the gate of the ranch.

My husband must have stepped a little too close to the entrance for their comfort because all at once lights and a recording came on saying we were trespassing and we must leave the premises immediately. So we did. It was one of the most exhilarating thrills of my life. I can actually say I was there. When my sister and I reviewed the pictures and video taken we couldn't believe we captured footage of an orb coming towards us and then circling back into the basin. Plus two bright lights shooting up into the sky was also seen on the video. We had no idea these strange anomalies had occurred while filming and never saw them until we watched the clip. There is no doubt in my mind that the infamous 512 acre ranch is a hotspot for the supernatural. Paranormal phenomena is real; either by extraterrestrials, Bigfoot or other unworldly beings.

I don't see dead people like in the movie SIXTH SENSE, but I do have a sixth sense when it comes to feeling their presence around me. I have felt their energy ever since I was a little girl. I believe in my heart I am somehow being touched by the spiritual world. Spirits or ghosts are lost souls and we are unable to see them because of a hidden veil; a shroud to keep up apart. But there are portals within this thin cloth that some have passed through and that is why we are living with the dead!

"A THIN LINE SEPARATES INSTEAD
WHEN LIVING WITH THE DEAD"
M.M.D

HAUNTED

Eyes in windows stare out into darkness
Shadows disappear where silence creaks
Footsteps upon stairs step out do hearken
Wanderers move within the walls to seek
Prancing, dancing, throughout the realm
Dancing, prancing, mid an essence helm

Luminous robes float surpassing the air
Dominion upon an estate entombs, story
Colorless forms trample, without a care
For their hideous deaths assumed, gory
Glowing, flowing winged rulers' abode
Flowing, glowing, phantoms of long ago

Bloodless souls groan in memory, olden
Echoes the remembrance cloak's sorrow
Their once breathing forever time stolen
Its door to the dead locks out tomorrow
Gliding, hiding in a threshold's dome
Hiding, gliding, ever a befitting home

Sweet odors of demise, perfumed spoors
Along the wood for worms thus hidden
Spirits travel to a world the living abhor
Once there children's laughter forbidden
Toiling, spoiling, its pestilence dwells
Spoiling, toiling, haunted gate into hell

2004

www.ingramcontent.com/pod-product-compliance
Lightning Source LLC
Chambersburg PA
CBHW021618120626
46545CB00001B/284